American Economic History
Before 1860

GOLDENTREE BIBLIOGRAPHIES
in American History

under the series editorship of
Arthur S. Link

American Economic History Before 1860

compiled by

George Rogers Taylor

Eleutherian Mills-Hagley Foundation

APPLETON-CENTURY-CROFTS

Educational Division

New York   MEREDITH CORPORATION

Copyright © 1969 by

MEREDITH CORPORATION

All rights reserved

This book, or parts thereof, must not be used or reproduced in any manner without written permission. For information address the publisher, Appleton-Century-Crofts, Educational Division, Meredith Corporation, 440 Park Avenue South, New York, N.Y. 10016.

619–1

Library of Congress Card Number: 70-79173

390-86750-0

PRINTED IN THE UNITED STATES OF AMERICA

Editor's Foreword

GOLDENTREE BIBLIOGRAPHIES IN AMERICAN HISTORY are designed to provide students, teachers, and librarians with ready and reliable guides to the literature of American History in all its remarkable scope and variety. Volumes in the series cover comprehensively the major periods in American history, while additional volumes are devoted to all important subjects.

Goldentree Bibliographies attempt to steer a middle course between the brief list of references provided in the average textbook and the long bibliography in which significant items are often lost in the sheer number of titles listed. Each bibliography is, therefore, selective, with the sole criterion for choice being the significance—and not the age—of any particular work. The result is bibliographies of all works, including journal articles and doctoral dissertations, that are still useful, without bias in favor of any particular historiographical school.

Each compiler is a scholar long associated, both in research and teaching, with the period or subject of his volume. All compilers have not only striven to accomplish the objective of this series but have also cheerfully adhered to a general style and format. However, each compiler has been free to define his field, make his own selections, and work out internal organization as the unique demands of his period or subject have seemed to dictate.

The single great objective of *Goldentree Bibliographies in American History* will have been achieved if these volumes help researchers and students to find their way to the significant literature of American history.

Arthur S. Link

Preface

AS AN INTERDISCIPLINARY subject economic history overlaps with economics and history and also with such diverse fields as political, sociological, technological, and even literary history. Consequently the construction of a bibliography in this area requires many difficult decisions. Only those items which emphasize economic history or at least contribute substantially to the subject are included. But some arbitrary judgments have proved unavoidable for the boundary lines are not always as clear-cut or logically defensible as could be desired.

The items chosen are arranged in categories convenient for student use. For the most part they have been listed in a single category even though their inclusion under a second or even third heading could be justified. It seemed wise, however, to limit the number of cross references for to include many duplicate listings might become confusing and would reduce the number of different items possible of inclusion within a manual of moderate size. If a first trial does not give the desired information, the student should turn to related categories.

For all books not of a general nature, the student must give careful attention to the division of the bibliography into three time periods. In pursuing a particular topic which overlaps two time periods he must bear in mind that most references appear only once and that each will be listed only in the earliest of the two periods for which it supplies substantial information. Thus a book presenting appreciable material on both "The Colonial Period" and "The Early National Period, 1775-1820," will ordinarily appear in the earlier period only. Similarly, items presenting important matter for "The Early National Period" as well as "The Era of Accelerated Growth, 1820-1860" will be included only in the earlier category.

An attempt has been made to include not only the most useful books but also a considerable number of the more important articles appearing in the scholarly journals. These latter have been selected for their substantial merit. Often they cover subjects not yet adequately treated in more extensive works. Recent publications are emphasized though earlier studies of enduring value are also shown. The bibliography lists no manuscript collections but does note a few key, unpublished dissertations. A few references to contemporary works are listed separately at

PREFACE

the beginning of most of the divisions of the bibliography, followed by asterisks. These brief lists of important works written at the time serve chiefly as illustrations of the contemporary materials available. For extensive information as to research materials the student will, of course, have to refer to more specialized manuals and guides.

G. R. T.

Abbreviations

Ag Hist	Agricultural History
Ala Hist Q	Alabama Historical Quarterly
Am Econ Rev	American Economic Review
Am Her	American Heritage
Am Hist Assn, Ann Rep	American Historical Association, Annual Report
Am Hist Rev	American Historical Review
Am Neptune	American Neptune
Am Q	American Quarterly
Am Q Rev	American Quarterly Review
Ark Hist Q	Arkansas Historical Quarterly
Bull Am Assn State Loc Hist	Bulletin of the American Association for State and Local History
Bull Bus Hist Soc	Bulletin, Business Historical Society
Bus Hist Rev	Business History Review
Can Hist Rev	Canadian Historical Review
Can J Econ Pol Sci	Canadian Journal of Economics and Political Science
Colum Univ Q	Columbia University Quarterly
Comp Stud Soc Hist	Comparative Studies in Society and History
Conn Hist Soc Bull	Connecticut Historical Society Bulletin
Cotton Hist Rev	Cotton History Review
Del Hist	Delaware History
Econ Dev Cult Change	Economic Development and Cultural Change
Econ Geog	Economic Geography
Econ Hist Rev	Economic History Review
Econ J	Economic Journal
Econ Pol Sci Ser (Wis)	Economics and Political Science Series, University of Wisconsin
Encyc Soc Sci	Encyclopedia of the Social Sciences
Eng Hist Rev	English Historical Review
Essex Inst Hist Coll	Essex Institute Historical Collections
Explo Entrep Hist	Explorations in Entrepreneurial History
Filson Club Hist Q	Filson Club History Quarterly
Ga Hist Q	Georgia Historical Quarterly
Geog Rev	Geographical Review
Har Econ Stud	Harvard Economic Studies
Har Hist Mono	Harvard Historical Monographs, Harvard University
Har Hist Stud	Harvard Historical Studies, Harvard University
His-Am Hist Rev	Hispanic-American Historical Review
Hist N H	History of New Hampshire
Huntington Lib Q	Huntington Library Quarterly

Ind Mag Hist	Indiana Magazine of History
Iowa J Hist Pol	Iowa Journal of History and Politics
J Am Hist	Journal of American History, formerly Mississippi Valley Historical Review
J Am Stat Assn	Journal, American Statistical Association
J Econ Bus Hist	Journal of Economic and Business History
J Econ Hist	Journal of Economic History
J Ill State Hist Soc	Journal of the Illinois State Historical Society
J Miss Hist	Journal of Mississippi History
J Neg Hist	Journal of Negro History
J Pol Econ	Journal of Political Economy
J S Hist	Journal of Southern History
J W	Journal of the West
Ky Hist Soc Reg	The Register of the Kentucky Historical Society
Labor Hist	Labor History
Land Econ	Land Economics
Md Hist Mag	Maryland Historical Magazine
Me Hist Soc Coll	Maine Historical Society Collections
Mich Hist	Michigan History
Minn Hist	Minnesota History
Minn Hist Soc Coll	Minnesota Historical Society Collections
Miss Val Hist Rev	Mississippi Valley Historical Review, continued as Journal of American History
Mo Hist Rev	Missouri Historical Review
N C Hist Rev	North Carolina Historical Review
N Eng Q	New England Quarterly
N J Hist	New Jersey History
N Y Hist	New York History
N Y Hist Soc Q	New York Historical Society Quarterly
Ohio Arch Hist Q	Ohio Archaeological and Historical Quarterly
Ohio Hist Q	Ohio Historical Quarterly
Oxford Econ Pap	Oxford Economic Papers
Pac Hist Rev	Pacific Historical Review
Pap New Haven Colony Hist Soc	Papers of the New Haven Colony Historical Society
Pap Proc Am Econ Rev	Papers and Proceedings, American Economic Review
Penn Hist	Pennsylvania History
Penn Mag Hist Biog	Pennsylvania Magazine of History and Biography
Pol Sci Q	Political Science Quarterly
Proc Am Ant Soc	Proceedings, American Antiquarian Society
Proc Am Philos Soc	Proceedings, American Philosophical Society
Proc Mass Hist Soc	Proceedings, Massachusetts Historical Society
Proc Miss Val Hist Assn	Proceedings, Mississippi Valley Historical Association
Proc N J Hist Soc	Proceedings, New Jersey Historical Society
Proc R I Hist Soc	Proceedings, Rhode Island Historical Society
Pub Col Soc Mass	Colonial Society of Massachusetts Publications
Pub Econ (Berk)	Publications in Economics, University of California at Berkeley

Q J Econ	Quarterly Journal of Economics
R I Hist	Rhode Island History
Rev Econ Stat	Review of Economics and Statistics
S Atl Q	South Atlantic Quarterly
S C Hist Genea Mag	South Carolina Historical and Genealogical Magazine
S C Hist Mag	South Carolina Historical Magazine
S Econ J	Southern Economic Journal
S W Hist Q	Southwestern Historical Quarterly
S W Soc Sci Q	Southwestern Social Science Quarterly
Scandinavian Econ Hist Rev	Scandinavian Economic Historical Review
Sci Monthly	The Science Monthly
Ser Hist (Penn)	Series in History, University of Pennsylvania
Ser Pol Econ Pub Law (Penn)	Series in Political Economy and Public Law, University of Pennsylvania
Smithsonian J Hist	Smithsonian Journal of History
Stud (Ind)	Studies, Indiana University
Stud (Me)	Studies, University of Maine
Stud (Mo)	Studies, University of Missouri
Stud Bus Hist (Har)	Studies in Business History, Harvard University
Stud Hist (Smith)	Studies in History, Smith College
Stud Hist Econ Pub Law (Colum)	Studies in History, Economics, and Public Law, Columbia University
Stud Hist Pol Sci (Hop)	Studies in Historical and Political Science, Johns Hopkins University
Stud Soc Sci (Ill)	Studies in the Social Sciences, University of Illinois
Stud Soc Sci Hist (Wis)	Studies in the Social Sciences and History, University of Wisconsin
Tech Cult	Technology and Culture
Tenn Hist Q	Tennessee Historical Quarterly
Textile Hist Rev	Textile History Review
Tran Conn Acad Arts Sci	Transactions, Connecticut Academy of Arts and Science
Tran Royal Hist Soc	Transactions of the Royal Historical Society
Tran Wis Acad Sci Arts Letters	Transactions, Wisconsin Academy of Science, Arts and Letters
Va Mag Hist Biog	Virginia Magazine of History and Biography
Vt Hist	Vermont History
W Penn Hist Mag	Western Pennsylvania Historical Magazine
W Va Hist	West Virginia History
Wm Mar Q	William and Mary Quarterly, a Magazine of Early American History
Worcester Hist Soc Pub	Worcester Historical Society Publications
Yale Rev	Yale Review

Note: Cross-references are to page (**Boldface**) and to item numbers (roman). Items marked by a dagger (†) are available in paperback edition at the time this bibliography goes to press. The publisher and compiler invite suggestions for additions to future editions of the bibliography.

Contents

Editor's Foreward	v
Preface	vii
Abbreviations	ix
I. General Bibliographies and Guides	1
II. Methods and Theories	2
1. *General* (for frontier interpretations see below)	2
2. *Stages of Development*	4
3. *The "New" Economic History*	5
III. General Studies	6
1. *Textbooks and Books of Readings*	6
2. *General Works*	7
3. *Population, Labor, and Immigration*	9
4. *Extractive Industry, Land, and the Frontier*	11
5. *Trade, Transportation, and Travel*	13
6. *Manufacturing, Industrial Organization, and Technology*	14
7. *Financial and Business Organization*	15
IV. The Colonial Period	16
1. *General Studies*	16
2. *Regional and Local Studies*	18
3. *Population, Immigration, and the Migration Westward*	19
4. *Agriculture and Land Ownership*	20
5. *Extractive Industry Other than Agriculture*	21
6. *Transportation*	22
7. *Commerce*	23
A. THE MERCHANTS	23
B. TRADE	24
8. *Industry*	26
9. *Labor*	27
10. *Financial Organization*	28
11. *Governmental Relationships*	30
A. PROMOTION AND REGULATION OF ECONOMIC DEVELOPMENT	30
B. ECONOMIC FACTORS IN POLITICAL DEVELOPMENT	31
V. The Early National Period, 1775-1820	33
1. *General Studies*	33
2. *Regional and Local Studies*	35

	3. *Urban Studies*	36
	4. *Population, Immigration, and Migration*	37
	5. *Extractive Industry, Land Policy, and the Frontier*	37
	6. *Transportation*	40
	7. *Commerce*	41
	8. *Manufacturing, Processing, and Building*	44
	9. *Labor*	47
	10. *Finance*	48
	A. PUBLIC FINANCE	48
	B. MONEY AND FINANCIAL INSTITUTIONS	49
	C. PRICES AND BUSINESS CONDITIONS	51
	11. *Corporations and Government-Business Relations*	51
	12. *Economic Aspects of Major Political Developments*	53
	A. THE REVOLUTION, 1776-1783	53
	B. THE CONFEDERATION AND THE ADOPTION OF THE CONSTITUTION, 1784-1789	54
	C. THE NEW NATION, 1790-1820	55
VI.	The Era of Accelerated Growth, 1820-1860	56
	1. *General Contemporary Materials*	56
	2. *Other General Studies*	56
	3. *State and Regional Studies*	57
	4. *Urban Studies*	59
	5. *Population, Immigration, and Migration*	60
	6. *Agriculture*	61
	7. *Public Land Policy, Land Speculation, and the Frontier*	63
	8. *Extractive Industry Other than Agriculture*	65
	9. *Transportation and Communication*	67
	A. GENERAL INCLUDING ROADS AND BRIDGES	67
	B. WATER TRANSPORTATION	69
	C. RAILROADS	71
	10. *Commerce*	73
	11. *Manufacturing*	75
	A. GENERAL INCLUDING TECHNOLOGY	75
	B. INDUSTRY STUDIES	76
	12. *Labor*	79
	A. GENERAL	79
	B. FREE LABOR: LIVING AND WORKING CONDITIONS	80
	C. SLAVERY	81
	13. *Public Finance*	82
	14. *Money and Banking*	83
	15. *Prices and Business Conditions*	85

16. *Capital, Corporate Securities, and Insurance*	86
17. *Business Organization and Marketing*	87
18. *Government and Business*	88
Notes	89
Index	95

I. General Bibliographies and Guides

1 American Economic Association. *Index of Economic Journals:* Vol I, 1886-1924, 279; Vol II, 1925-1939, 470; Vol III, 1940-1949, 467; Vol IV, 1950-1954, 389; Vol V, 1954-1959, 533; and Vol VI, 1960–1963, 552. Homewood, Ill.: Vols I, II, and III pub 1961; Vols IV and V, 1962; Vol VI, 1965.

2 American Economic Association. *The Journal of Economic Abstracts.* Vol I, 1963 to date.

3 American Historical Association. Service Center for Teachers, Washington, D.C., publishes a pamphlet series providing bibliographic guides. Many of these, for example, *The American Frontier* by Ray A. Billington and *The Development of American Labor* by Albert A. Blum, are useful to students of American economic history.

4 BRIGHAM, Clarence S. *History and Bibliography of American Newspapers, 1690-1820.* Worcester, Mass., 1947.

5 CAVE, Alfred A. *Jacksonian Democracy and the Historians.* Mono (Fla). Gainesville, Fla., 1964.

6 CLARK, Thomas D., ed. *Travels in the Old South: A Bibliography.* 3 vols. Norman, Okla., 1956-1959.

7 DANIELLS, Lorna M., comp. *Studies in Enterprise: A Selected Bibliography of American and Canadian Company Histories and Biographies of Businessman.* Boston, 1957.

8 DRAKE, Milton, comp. *Almanacs of the United States.* 2 vols. New York, 1962.

9 EDWARDS, Everett E., comp. *A Bibliography of the History of Agriculture in the United States.* Washington, D.C., 1930.

10 EDWARDS, Everett E., comp. *References on American Colonial Agriculture.* Washington, D.C., 1938.

11 FERGUSON, Eugene S. "Contributions to Bibliography in the History of Technology." *Tech Cult,* III (1962), 73-84, 167-174, 298-306; IV (1963), 318-330; V (1964), 416-434, 578-594; VI (1965), 99-107.

12 GOODRICH, Carter. "Recent Contributions to Economic History: The United States, 1789-1860." *J Econ Hist,* XIX (1959), 25-43.

13 HARPER, Lawrence A. "Recent Contributions to American Economic History: American History to 1789." *J Econ Hist,* XIX (1959), 1-24.

14 HASSE, A. R. comp. *Index of Economic Material in Documents of the States of the United States.* 13 vols. Washington, D.C., 1907-1922.

15 HUBACH, Robert R., ed. *Early Midwestern Travel Narratives: An Annotated Bibliography, 1634-1850.* Detroit, 1961.†

16 HUTCHINS, John G. B. "Recent Contributions to Business History: The United States." *J Econ Hist,* XIX (1959), 103-121.

17 LARSON, Henrietta M., comp. *Guide to Business History.* Cambridge, Mass., 1950.

18 MUGRIDGE, Donald H. and Blanche P. MC CRUM. *A Guide to the Study of the United States of America: Respretnative Books Reflecting the Development of American Life and Thought.* Washington, 1960.

19 MUNN, Robert F. *The Coal Industry in America: A Bibliography and Guide to Studies.* Morgantown, W. Va., 1965.

20 NELSON, Daniel, comp. *A Checklist of Writings on the Economic History of the Greater Philadelphia-Wilmington Region.* Wilmington, Del., 1968.

1 REEVES, Dorothea D. *Resources for the Study of Economic History, a Preliminary Guide to Pre-twentieth Century Printed Materials in Collections Located in Certain American and British Libraries.* Cambridge, Mass., 1961.

2 ROSE, F. D. *American Labor in Journals of History: A Bibliography.* Champaign, Ill., 1962.

3 SCHLEIFFER, Hedwig and Ruth CRANDALL, comps. *Index to Economic History: Essays in Festschriften, 1900-1950.* Cambridge, Mass., 1953.

4 STOKES, Issac N. *The Iconography of Manhattan Island, 1498–1909.* 6 vols. New York, 1915-1928.

5 United States Department of the Interior. *Public Lands Bibliography.* Washington, D.C., 1962.

6 WHITEHILL, Walter Muir. *The Arts in Early American History: Needs and Opportunities for Study.* Chapel Hill, 1965.

II. Methods and Theories

1. General

7 ABRAMOVITZ, Moses. "Long Swings in United States Economic Growth." *38th Annual Report of the National Bureau of Economic Research.* New York, 1958, 47-56.

8 ABRAMOVITZ, Moses. "The Nature and Significance of Kuznets Cycles." *Econ Dev Cult Change*, IX (1961), 225-248.

9 AITKEN, Hugh G. J. "On the Present State of Economic History." *Can J Econ Pol Sci*, XXVI (1960), 87-95.

10 ASHLEY, W. J. "On the Study of Economic History." *Q J Econ*, VII (1893), 115-136.

11 ASHTON, T. S. "The Relation of Economic History to Theory." *Economica*, ns, XIII (1946), 81-96.

12 BARDHAN, Pranab. "External Economics, Economic Development, and the Theory of Protection." *Oxford Econ Pap*, ns, XVI (1964), 40-54.

13 BROUDE, Henry W. "The Significance of Regional Studies for the Elaboration of National Economic History." *J Econ Hist*, XX (1960), 588-596.

14 CLAPHAM, Sir John. "Economic History as a Discipline." *Encyc Soc Sci*, V (1930), 327-330.

15 CLARK, A. H. "Geographical Change: A Theme for Economic History." *J Econ Hist*, XX (1960), 607-613.

16 CLARK, Colin. *The Conditions of Economic Progress.* 3d ed. New York, 1957.

17 COCHRAN, Thomas C. "The Economics in Business History." *J Econ Hist*, V (1945), 54-65.

18 COCHRAN, Thomas C, "The Entrepreneur in American Capital Formation," in *Capital Formation and Economic Growth.* By Universities-National Bureau Committee for Economic Research. Princeton, 1955, 339-373.

METHODS AND THEORIES 3

1 COLE, Arthur H. "Business History and Economic History." *J Econ Hist,* V (1945), 45-53.
2 COLE, Arthur H. "Meso-economics: A Contribution from Entrepreneurial History." *Explo Entrep Hist,* 2d ser, VI (1968), 3-33.
3 EASTERLIN, Richard A. "Economic–Demographic Interactions and Long Swings in Economic Growth." *Am Econ Rev,* LVI (1966), 1063-1104. (Explains the rationale of long swings or Kuznets cycles. Extensive bibliographical references.)
4 FABRICANT, S. "Study of the Size and Efficiency of the American Economy." *Economic Consequences of the Size of Nations.* Ed. E. A. G. Robinson. New York, 1960, 35-53.
5 GALAMBOS, Louis. "Business History and the Theory of the Growth of the Firm." *Explo Entrep Hist,* 2d ser, IV (1966), 3-16.
6 GERSCHENKRON, Alexander. *Continuity in History and other Essays.* Cambridge, Mass., 1968.
7 GLADE, William P. "Approaches to a Theory of Entrepreneurial Formation." *Explo Entrep Hist,* 2d ser, IV (1967), 245-259.
8 HARTWELL, R. M. "The Causes of the Industrial Revolution: An Essay in Methodology." *Econ Hist Rev,* 2d ser, XVIII (1965), 164-182.
9 HIRSCHMAN, Albert O. *The Strategy of Economic Development.* New Haven, 1958.†
10 HOOVER, Edgar M. *The Location of Economic Activity.* New York, 1948.†
11 HUGHES, H. Stuart. "The Historian and the Social Scientist." *Am Hist Rev,* LXVI (1960), 20-46.
12 ISARD, Walter, et al. *Methods of Regional Analysis.* New York, 1960.
13 KUZNETS, Simon. *Economic Change: Selected Essays in Business Cycles, National Income, and Economic Growth.* 1st ed. New York, 1953.
14 MC CLELLAND, David C. *The Achieving Society.* Princeton, 1961.†
15 MEIER, Gerald M. *Leading Issues in Development Economics.* New York, 1964.
16 NORTH, Douglass C. "Location Theory and Regional Economic Growth." *J Pol Econ,* LXIII (1955), 243-258.
17 REDLICH, Fritz. "Economic Development, Entrepreneurship, and Psychologism: A Social Scientists Critique of McClelland's *Achieving Society.*" *Explo Entrep Hist,* 2d ser, I (1963), 10-35.
18 ROBINSON, E. A. G., ed. *Economic Consequences of the Size of Nations.* New York, 1960. (The introduction by Robinson summarizes the general problem and the item by S. Fabricant, see **3.4**, 35-53, raises interesting questions for the U.S.)
19 SCHUMPETER, J. A. "The Creative Response in Economic History." *J Econ Hist,* VII (1947), 149-159.
20 SELIGMAN, E. R. A. *The Economic Interpretation of History.* New York, 1912.†
21 SIRKIN, Gerald. "The Theory of the Regional Economic Base." *Rev Econ Stat,* XLI (1959), 426-429.

1 STIGLER, George J. "The Division of Labour is Limited by the Extent of the Market." *J Pol Econ,* LIX (1951), 185-193.
2 STRASSMANN, W. Paul. "Creative Destruction and Partial Obsolescence in American Economic Development." *J Econ Hist,* XIX (1959), 335-349.
3 TIEBOUT, Charles M. "Exports and Regional Economic Growth." *J Pol Econ,* LXIV (1956), 160-169. (Includes a reply by Douglass C. North and a rejoinder by the author.)
4 WATKINS, M. H. "A Staple Theory of Economic Growth." *Can J Econ Pol Sci,* XXIX (1963), 141-158.
5 WILLIAMSON, Harold F. "Business History and Economic History." *J Econ Hist,* XXVI (1966), 407-417.
6 WOHL, R. R., ed. *Change and the Entrepreneur: Postulates and Patterns for Entrepreneurial History.* Cambridge, Mass., 1949.

2. Stages of Development

7 BARAN, Paul and Ernest HOBSBAWM. "The Stages of Economic Growth: A Review." *Kyklos,* XIV (1961), 234-242. (A socialist criticism of Rostow's stages doctrine.)
8 BAUDET, H. and J. H. van STUIJVENBERG. "Rostow's Theory on Growth." *Weltwirtschaftliches Archiv,* XC (1963), 57-76.
9 FISHLOW, Albert. "Empty Economic Stages?" *Econ J,* LXXV (1965), 112-125.
10 GRAS, N. S. B. "The Rise and Development of Economic History." *Econ Hist Rev,* I (1927), 12-34.
11 GRAS, N. S. B. "Stages in Economic History." *J Econ Bus Hist,* II (1930), 395-418.
12 ISARD, Walter. *Location and Space-Economy.* Boston, 1956.
13 KUZNETS, Simon. "Notes on the Take-Off." See **4.20,** 22-43.
14 MYRDAL, Gunnar. "The Theories of 'Stages of Growth.'" *Scandinavian Econ Hist Rev,* 2d ser, XV (1967), 1-12.
15 OHLIN, Goran. "Reflections on the Rostow Doctrine." *Econ Dev Cult Change,* IX (1961), 648-655.
16 ROSOVSKY, Henry. "The Take-Off into Sustained Controversy." *J Econ Hist,* XXV (1965), 271-275.
17 ROSTOW, W. W. "Industrialization and Economic Growth," in *First International Conference of Economic History.* Stockholm, 1960, 17-34.
18 ROSTOW, W. W. *Process of Economic Growth.* 2d ed. Oxford, 1960.†
19 ROSTOW, W. W. *The Stages of Economic Growth.* Cambridge, Mass., 1960.†
20 ROSTOW, W. W., ed. *The Economics of Take-Off into Sustained Growth.* Proceedings of a Conference held by the International Economic Association. New York, 1965. (A symposium on the Rostow doctrine. For Rostow's statement see pp 1-21.)

3. The "New" Economic History

1 BRUCHEY, Stuart. "Douglass C. North on American Economic Growth." *Explo Entrep Hist,* 2d ser, I (1964), 145-158.

2 CHAMBERS, E. J. and D. F. GORDON. "Primary Products and Economic Growth: An Empirical Measurement." *J Pol Econ,* LXXIV (1966), 315-332.

3 CONRAD, Alfred H. "Econometrics and Southern History." *Explo Entrep Hist,* 2d ser, VI (1968), 34-53. With comments by R. W. Fogel, 54-58; Stuart Bruchey, 59-65. and Alfred D. Chandler Jr., 66-74.

4 CONRAD, Alfred H. and John R. MEYER. *The Economics of Slavery and Other Studies in Econometric History.* Chicago, 1964.

5 DAVIS, Lance E. "And It Will Never Be Literature." *Explo Entrep Hist,* 2d ser. VI (1968), 75-92.

6 DAVIS, Lance E. "Professor Fogel and the New Economic History." *Econ Hist Rev,* 2d ser, XIX (1966), 657-663.

7 DAVIS, Lance E., J. R. T. HUGHES, and S. REITER. "Aspects of Quantitative Research in Economic History." *J Econ Hist,* XX (1960), 539-547.

8 DESAI, Meghnad J. "Some Issues in Econometric History." *Econ Hist Rev,* 2d ser, XXI (1968), 1-16.

9 FOGEL, R. W. "The New Economic History: Its Findings and Methods." *Econ Hist Rev,* 2d ser, XIX (1966), 642-656.

10 FOGEL, R. W. "A Provisional View of the 'New Economic History.'" *Am Econ Rev,* LIV (1964), 377-389.

11 FOGEL, R. W. *Railroads and American Economic Growth. Stud Hist Pol Sci* (Hop). Baltimore, 1964.

12 FOGEL, R. W. "The Reunification of Economic History with Economic Theory." *Pap Proc Am Econ Rev,* LV (1965), 92-98.

13 GOODRICH, Carter. "Economic History: One Field or Two?" *J Econ Hist,* XX (1960), 531-538.

14 HACKER, Louis M. "The New Revolution in Economic History: A Review Article Based on *Railroads and Economic Growth* by R. W. Fogel." *Explo Entrep Hist,* 2d ser, III (1966), 159-175.

15 HUGHES, J. R. T. "Fact and Theory in Economic History." *Explo Entrep Hist,* 2d ser, III (1966), 75-100.

16 HUNT, E. H. "The New Economic History: Professor Fogel's Study of American Railways." *History,* LIII (1968), 3-18. With comment by G. R. Hawk, 18-23.

17 HUNT, E. H. "Railroad Social Saving in Nineteenth Century America." *Am Econ Rev,* LVII (1967), 909-910.

18 MC CLELLAND, Peter D. "Railroads, American Growth, and the New Economic History: A Critique." *J Econ Hist,* XXVIII (1968), 102-123.

19 MEYER, John R. and Alfred H. CONRAD. "Economic Theory, Statistical Inference and Economic History." *J Econ Hist,* XVII (1957), 524-544.

1 MURPHY, George G. S. "The 'New' History." *Explo Entrep Hist*, 2d ser, II (1965), 132-146.
2 NERLOVE, Marc. "Railroads and American Economic Growth." *J Econ Hist*, XXVI (1966), 107-115. (A review of Fogel's *Railroads and American Economic Growth.*)
3 NORTH, Douglass C. "Comments on Stuart Bruchey's Paper." *Explo Entrep Hist*, 2d ser, I (1964), 159-163.
4 NORTH, Douglass C. "Quantitative Research in American Economic History." *Am Econ Rev*, LIII (1963), 128-130.
5 NORTH, Douglass C. "The State of Economic History." *Pap Proc Am Econ Rev*, LV (1965), 86-91.
6 REDLICH, Fritz. "'New' and Traditional Approaches to Economic History and Their Interdependence." *J Econ Hist*, XXV (1965), 480-495.
7 REDLICH, Fritz. "Potentialities and Pitfalls in Economic History." *Explo Entrep Hist*, 2d ser, VI (1968), 109-115.
8 RUBIN, Julius. "Review of R. W. Fogel's *Railroads and American Economic Growth.*" *Tech Cult*, VIII (1967), 228-234.
9 SCHEIBER, Harry N. "On the New Economic History—and Its Limitations: A Review Essay." *Ag Hist*, XLI (1967), 383-395.
10 TUNZELMANN, G. N. Von. "The New Economic History: An Econometric Appraisal." *Explo Entrep Hist*, 2d ser, V (1968), 175-200.

III. General Studies

1. Textbooks and Books of Readings

11 ANDREANO, Ralph L., ed. *New Views on American Economic Development.* Cambridge, Mass., 1965.†
12 BINING, Arthur C. *The Rise of American Economic Life.* Rev by Thomas C. Cochran. New York, 1964.
13 BOLINO, August C. *The Development of the American Economy.* Columbus, 1966.
14 BRUCHEY, Stuart. *The Roots of American Economic Growth, 1607-1861.* New York, 1965.†
15 CALLENDER, Guy Stevens, ed. *Selections from the Economic History of the United States, 1765-1860.* Boston, 1909. (Especially valued for the introductory statements by the editor.)
16 CHANDLER, Alfred D. Jr., Stuart BRUCHEY, and L. GALAMBOS, eds. *The Changing Economic Order: Readings in American Business and Economic History.* New York, 1968.
17 CLOUGH, Shepard B. and Theodore MARBURG. *The Economic Basis of American Civilization.* New York, 1968.
18 COCHRAN, Thomas C. and Thomas B. BREWER, eds. *Views of American Economic Growth.* 2 vols. New York, 1966.

GENERAL STUDIES

1 COMMONS, John R., et al., eds. *A Documentary History of American Industrial Society.* 10 vols. New York, 1909-1911. Repr with new introductions. New York, 1958.

2 DAVIS, Lance E., J. R. T. HUGHES, and D. M. MC DOUGALL. *American Economic History.* 2d rev ed. Homewood, Ill., 1965.

3 FAULKNER, Harold U. *American Economic History.* 8th ed. New York, 1960. (Now undergoing general revision.)

4 FITE, Gilbert C. and Jim E. REESE. *An Economic History of the United States.* 2d ed. Boston, 1965.

5 GLAAB, Charles N., ed. *The American City: A Documentary History.* Homewood, Ill., 1963.†

6 HACKER, Louis M. *The Triumph of American Capitalism.* New York, 1946.†

7 HARRIS, Seymour E. *American Economic History.* New York, 1961.

8 JONES, Peter d'a. *America's Wealth: The Economic History of an Open Society.* New York, 1963.†

9 KIRKLAND, Edward C. *A History of American Economic Life.* 3d ed. New York, 1951. (This standard text is now being revised by the author.)

10 KROOSS, Herman E. *American Economic Development.* 2d ed. Englewood Cliffs, N. J., 1965.

11 LANE, Frederic C. and Jelle C. RIEMERSMA, eds. *Enterprise and Secular Change: Readings in Economic History.* Homewood, Ill., 1953.

12 NORTH, Douglass C. *The Economic Growth of the United States, 1790-1860.* Englewood Cliffs, N.J., 1961.†

13 NORTH, Douglass C. *Growth and Welfare in the American Past.* Englewood Cliffs, N.J., 1966.†

14 NORTH, Douglass C. and Robert P. THOMAS, eds. *The Growth of the American Economy to 1860.* New York, 1968.

15 ROBERTSON, Ross M. *History of the American Economy.* 2d ed. New York, 1964.

16 ROBERTSON, Ross M. and James L. PATE, eds. *Readings in United States Economic and Business History.* Boston, 1966.†

17 SCHEIBER, Harry N., ed. *United States Economic History: Selected Readings.* New York, 1964.†

18 SOULE, George and Vincent P. CAROSSO. *American Economic History.* New York, 1957.

19 SUPPLE, Barry E., ed. *Experience of Economic Growth: Case Studies in Economic History.* New York, 1963.†

20 WILLIAMSON, Harold F., ed. *Growth of the American Economy.* 2d ed. New York, 1951.

21 WRIGHT, Chester W. *Economic History of the United States.* New York, 1949.

2. General Works

22 ABRAMOVITZ, Moses. "Employment, Growth and Price Levels." See 9.11, 411-466. (An analysis of long-run swings in economic growth.)

GENERAL STUDIES

1 AITKEN, Hugh G. J., ed. *Explorations in Enterprise.* Cambridge, Mass., 1965. (Essays analyzing the role of the entrepreneur.)
2 ANDERSON, C. Arnold and Mary Jean BOWMAN, eds. *Education and Economic Development.* Chicago, 1965.
3 BALLAGH, James C., ed. *Economic History, 1607-1865.* Vol V of *The South in the Building of the Nation.* Richmond, 1910.
4 BREBNER, John Bartlet. *North Atlantic Triangle: The Interplay of Canada, the United States and Great Britain.* New York, 1945.†
5 BREMNER, Robert H. *American Philanthropy.* Chicago, 1960.†
6 COCHRAN, Thomas C. "The History of a Business Society." *J Am Hist,* LIV (1967), 5-18.
7 COLE, Arthur H. *Business Enterprise and Its Social Setting.* Cambridge, Mass., 1959.
8 DILLARD, Dudley. *Economic Development of the North Atlantic Community.* Englewood Cliffs, N.J., 1967.
9 DORFMAN, Joseph. *The Economic Mind in American Civilization, 1606-1933.* 5 vols. New York, 1946-1959.
10 EATON, Clement. *A History of the Old South.* New York, 1966.
11 *Facts and Factors in Economic History: Articles by Former Students of Edwin Francis Gay.* Cambridge, Mass., 1932. Repr New York, 1967.
12 GARBER, John P. *The Valley of the Delaware and Its Place in American History.* Philadelphia, 1934. (See chap viii.)
13 GLAAB, Charles N. and A. Theodore BROWN. *A History of Urban America.* New York, 1967.†
14 GOLDSMITH, Raymond W. "Employment, Growth and Price Levels." See 9.11, 267-279. (An important analysis of long-term trends in national product and income.)
15 GREENHUT, Melvin L. and W. Tate WHITMAN. *Essays in Southern Economic Development.* Chapel Hill, 1964.
16 HAWK, Emory Q. *Economic History of the South.* New York, 1934.
17 HOGAN, William R. *The Texas Republic: A Social and Economic History.* Norman, Okla., 1946.
18 HUGHES, J. R. T. *The Vital Few: American Economic Progress and Its Protagonists.* Boston, 1966. (Includes essays on William Penn, Eli Whitney, and Brigham Young.)†
19 KUZNETS, Simon. *Economic Growth and Structure: Selected Essays.* New York, 1965.
20 KUZNETS, Simon. *Modern Economic Growth: Rate, Structure, and Spread.* New Haven, 1966.†
21 LAMPARD, Eric E. *Industrial Revolution: Interpretations and Perspectives.* Washington, D.C., 1957.†
22 MARX, Leo. *The Machine in the Garden: Technology and the Pastoral Ideal in America.* New York, 1967.†
23 MILLER, William, ed. *Men in Business: Essays in History of Entrepreneurship.* Cambridge. Mass., 1952.†

GENERAL STUDIES

9

1 MYERS, Gustavus. *History of the Great American Fortunes.* 3 vols. Chicago, 1911.

2 PERLOFF, Harvey S., Edgar S. DUNN, Jr., Eric E. LAMPARD, and Richard F. MUTH. *Regions, Resources, and Economic Growth.* Baltimore, 1960. (See chap x.)†

3 REZNECK, Samuel. "The Rise and Early Development of Industrial Consciousness in the United States, 1760-1830." *J Econ Bus Hist,* IV (1932), 784-811.

4 SALE, Randall D. and Edwin D. KARN. *American Expansion: A Book of Maps.* Homewood, Ill., 1967.†

5 SCHNEIDER, David M. *The History of Public Welfare in New York State, 1609-1866.* Chicago, 1938.

6 SLICHTER, Sumner H. *Economic Growth in the United States: Its History, Problems and Prospects.* Baton Rouge, 1961.†

7 TANG, Anthony M. *Economic Development in the Southern Piedmont, 1860-1950.* Chapel Hill, 1958. (See chap ii for an interesting interpretation of the pre-1860 period.)

8 TAYLOR, George Rogers. "American Economic Growth before 1840: An Exploratory Essay." *J Econ Hist,* XXIV (1964), 427-444.

9 THOMPSON, Wilbur R. *A Preface to Urban Economics.* Baltimore, 1965.

10 United States Bureau of the Census. *Historical Statistics of the United States, Colonial Times to 1957.* Washington, D.C., 1960.

11 United States Congress, Joint Economic Committee, 86th Congress, 1st Session, *Hearings,* Part 2, "Historical and Comparative Rates of Production, Productivity and Prices." Washington, D.C., 1959. (For a reprint see **6.11**, 337-361.)

12 WHITEHILL, Walter Muir. *Boston: A Topographical History.* Cambridge, Mass., 1959.

13 YOUNG, James H. *The Toadstool Millionaires: A Social History of Patent Medicines in America before Federal Regulation.* Princeton, 1961.

3. Population, Labor, and Immigration

14 CHICKERING, Jesse. *A Statistical View of the Population of Massachusetts from 1765 to 1840.* Boston, 1846.

* * * * * * *

15 BEARD, Mary. *The American Labor Movement: A Short History.* New York, 1937.

16 BESTOR, Arthur E., Jr. *Backwoods Utopias: The Sectarian and Owenite Phases of Communitarian Socialism in America, 1663-1829.* Philadelphia, 1950.

17 BIMBA, Anthony. *The History of the American Working Class.* New York, 1933.

18 COMMONS, John R., et al. *History of Labour in the United States.* 4 vols. New York, 1921-1935.

19 CONRAD, Alfred H., et al. "Slavery as an Obstacle to Economic Growth in the United States: A Panel Discussion." *J Econ Hist,* XXVII (1967), 518-560.

10 GENERAL STUDIES

1 CONRAD, Alfred H. and John R. MEYER. *The Economics of Slavery and Other Studies in Econometric History.* Chicago, 1964.
2 DAVIS, David Brion. *The Problem of Slavery in Western Culture.* Ithaca, 1966.
3 DU BOIS, W. E. B. *The Suppression of the African Slave-Trade to the United States of America, 1638-1870.* New York, 1896.
4 DULLES, Foster Rhea. *Labor in America.* 2d rev ed. New York, 1960.
5 FONER, Philip S. *History of the Labor Movement in the United States.* New York, 1955.
6 GENOVESE, Eugene D. *The Political Economy of Slavery.* New York, 1965.†
7 GLASS, D. V. and D. E. C. EVERSLEY, eds. *Population in History: Essays in Historical Demography.* Chicago, 1965.
8 HANDLIN, Oscar, ed. *Immigration as a Factor in American History.* Englewood Cliffs, N.J., 1959.†
9 HANSEN, M. L. *The Atlantic Migration, 1607-1860.* Cambridge, Mass., 1940.†
10 HERRICK, Cheesman A. *White Servitude in Pennsylvania: Indentured and Redemption Labor in Colony and Commonwealth.* Philadelphia, 1926.
11 JONES, Maldwyn A. *American Immigration.* Chicago, 1960.†
12 KLEIN, Herbert S. *Slavery in the Americas: A Comparative Study of Virginia and Cuba.* Chicago, 1967.
13 KUCZYNSKI, Jürgen. *A Short History of Labour Conditions under Industrial Capitalism.* 4 vols. 2d ed. New York, 1943-1946.
14 NEUFELD, Maurice. *A Representative Bibliography of American Labor History.* Ithaca, 1964.
15 PHILLIPS, Ulrich B. *American Negro Slavery.* New York, 1918. Repr New York, 1966.†
16 POTTER, J. "The Growth of Population in America, 1700-1860."See **10.7**, 631-688.
17 RAYBACK, Joseph G. *A History of American Labor.* New York, 1959.†
18 STROUD, Gene S. and Gilbert E. DONAHUE, comps. *Labor History in the United States: A General Bibliography.* Urbana, 1961.
19 THOMPSON, Warren S. and P. K. WHELPTON. *Population Trends in the United States.* New York, 1933.
20 United States Bureau of the Census. *A Century of Population Growth... 1790-1900.* Washington, D.C., 1909.
21 United States Bureau of the Census. *Sixteenth Census, 1940, I, Population.* Washington, D.C., 1942. (Provides detailed statistics on urban growth from 1790.)
22 United States Bureau of Labor Statistics. *History of Wages in the United States from Colonial Times to 1928.* Bull 499. Washington, D.C., 1929.
23 WITTKE, Carl F. *We Who Built America.* New York, 1939.†
24 WOODMAN, Harold D., ed. *Slavery and the Southern Economy.* New York, 1966.†

1 WRIGHT, Carroll D. *History and Growth of the United States Census.* Washington, D.C., 1900.

2 ZILVERSMIT, Arthur. *The First Emancipation: The Abolition of Slavery in the North.* Chicago. 1967.

4. Extractive Industry, Land, and the Frontier

3 ADAMS, Ramon F. *The Rampaging Herd: A Bibliography... on Men and Events in the Cattle Industry.* Norman, Okla., 1959.

4 ALBION, Robert G. *Forests and Sea Power: The Timber Problem of the Royal Navy, 1652-1862.* Cambridge, Mass., 1926.

5 BIDWELL, Percy W. and John I. FALCONER. *History of Agriculture in the Northern United States, 1620-1860.* New York, 1941.

6 BILLINGTON, Ray A. *America's Frontier Heritage.* New York, 1966.†

7 BILLINGTON, Ray A. *Westward Expansion: A History of the American Frontier.* New York, 1967. (Numerous editions.)

8 BONNER, James C. *A History of Georgia Agriculture, 1732-1860.* Athens, Ga., 1964.

9 BRUCE, Kathleen, *Virginia Iron Manufacture in the Slave Era.* New York, 1931.

10 BRUCHEY, Stuart, ed. *Cotton and the Growth of the American Economy, 1790-1860.* New York, 1967.†

11 CLARK, Thomas D. *Frontier America: The Story of the Westward Movement.* New York, 1959.

12 CLAWSON, Marion. *The Land System of the United States: An Introduction to the History and Practice of Land Use and Land Tenure.* Lincoln, Neb., 1968.

13 CLEMEN, Alexander. *The American Livestock and Meat Industry.* NewYork, 1923.

14 DAY, Clarence A. *A History of Maine Agriculture, 1604-1860.* Orono, Me., 1954.

15 DEFEBAUGH, James E. *History of the Lumber Industry of America.* 2 vols. Chicago, 1906-1907.

16 DEMAREE, A. L. *The American Agricultural Press, 1819-1860.* New York, 1941.

17 FLETCHER, S. W. *Pennsylvania Agriculture and Country Life, 1640-1840.* Harrisburg, 1950.

18 FOX, William F. *A History of the Lumber Industry in the State of New York.* Washington, D.C., 1902.

19 GATES, Paul W. "Research in the History of American Land Tenure." *Ag Hist,* XXVIII (1954), 121-126.

20 GOODE, George B., et al. *The Fisheries and Fishery Industries of the United States.* Washington, D.C., 1884-1887.

21 GRAY, Lewis C. *History of Agriculture in the Southern United States to 1860.* 2 vols. Washington, D.C., 1933.

GENERAL STUDIES

1. HAMMOND, M. B. *The Cotton Industry.* New York, 1897.

2. HEDRICK, Ulysses P. *A History of Agriculture in the State of New York.* Albany, 1933.†

3. HEDRICK, Ulysses P. *A History of Horticulture in America to 1860.* New York, 1950.

4. HOHMAN, Elmo P. *The American Whaleman: A Study of Life and Labor in the Whaling Industry.* New York, 1928.

5. INNIS, Harold A. *The Cod Fisheries: The History of an International Economy.* New Haven, 1940.

6. KLOSE, Nelson. *A Concise Study Guide to the American Frontier.* Lincoln, Neb., 1967.†

7. MC FARLAND, Raymond. *A History of the New England Fisheries.* Philadelphia, 1911.

8. MORGAN, Dale L. "The Fur Trade and Its Historians." *Minn Hist,* XL (1966), 151-156.

9. PAXSON, Frederic L. *History of the American Frontier, 1763-1893.* New York, 1924.

10. PHILBRICK, Francis S. *The Rise of the West, 1754-1830.* New York, 1965.†

11. PHILLIPS, Ulrich B., ed. *Plantation and Frontier.* See 7.1, vols I and II.

12. ROBERT, Joseph C. *The Story of Tobacco in America.* New York, 1949. Repr Chapel Hill, 1966.†

13. ROSENBERRY, Lois (Kimball) Mathews. *The Expansion of New England.* New York, 1962.

14. SAKOLSKI, A. M. *The Great American Land Bubble.* New York, 1932.

15. SCHMIDT, Louis B. and E. D. ROSS. *Readings in the Economic History of American Agriculture.* New York, 1925.

16. SCHULTZ, Theodore. *Transforming Traditional Agriculture.* New Haven, 1964.†

17. SITTERSON, J. Carlyle. *Sugar Country: The Cane Sugar Industry in the South, 1753-1950.* Lexington, Ky., 1953.

18. TAYLOR, Paul S. "Plantation Agriculture in the United States: Seventeenth to Twentieth Centuries." *Land Econ,* XXX (1954), 141-152.

19. THOMPSON, James W. *A History of Livestock Raising in the United States, 1607-1860.* Agricultural History Series No. 5, U.S. Dept. of Agriculture. Washington, D.C., 1942.

20. TOWER, Walter S. *A History of the American Whale Fishery. Ser Pol Econ Pub Law* (Penn). Philadelphia, 1907.

21. WEBB, Walter P. *The Great Frontier.* Austin, 1964.

22. WOODWARD, Carl R. *The Development of Agriculture in New Jersey, 1640-1880.* New Brunswick, 1927.

GENERAL STUDIES

5. Trade, Transportation, and Travel

1 AMBLER, Charles H. *A History of Transportation in the Ohio Valley.* Glendale, Calif., 1932.

2 BATES, William W. *American Marine: The Shipping Question in History and Politics.* Boston, 1893.

3 BERRILL, K. "International Trade and the Rate of Economic Growth." *Econ Hist Rev,* 2d ser, XII (1960), 351-359.

4 CRAIB, Roderick H. *A Picture History of U.S. Transportation: On Rails, Roads, and Rivers.* New York, 1958.

5 DOLAN, J. R. *The Yankee Peddlers of Early America.* New York, 1964.

6 EVANS, Charles H., comp. *Exports, Domestic and Foreign, from the American Colonies to Great Britain, from 1697-1787, Inclusive and Exports, Domestic and Foreign, from the United States to All Countries, from 1789 to 1883, Inclusive.* House Miscl. Docs., 48 cong., 1 Sess., No. 49, pt. 2. Serial no. 2236. Washington, D.C., 1884.

7 HARRIMAN, D. G. *American Tariffs from Plymouth Rock to McKinley.* New York, 1892.

8 HOMANS, Isaac Smith. *A Cyclopedia of Commerce and Commercial Navigation.* Ed. by J. Smith Homans and J. Smith, Jr. New York, 1858.

9 HOMANS, Isaac Smith. *An Historical and Statistical Account of the Foreign Commerce of the United States.* Comp. by J. Smith Homans, Jr. New York, 1857. Repr New York, 1956.

10 HORNUNG, C. P. *Wheels Across America: A Pictorial Cavalcade Illustrating the Early Development of Vehicular Transportation.* New York, 1959.

11 HULBERT, Archer B. *Historic Highways of America.* 16 vols. Cleveland, 1902-1905.

12 HULBERT, Archer B. *The Paths of Inland Commerce: A Chronicle of Trail, Road, and Waterway.* New Haven, 1920.

13 JOHNSON, Emory R., et al. *History of Domestic and Foreign Commerce in the United States.* 2 vols. Washington, D.C., 1915. Repr Washington, D.C., 1922.

14 LANE, Wheaton J. *From Indian Trail to Iron Horse: Travel and Transportation in New Jersey, 1620-1860.* Princeton, 1939.

15 LIPPINCOTT, Isaac. *Internal Trade of the United States, 1700-1860.* Chicago, 1916.

16 LOVE, W. De Loss. "The Navigation of the Connecticut River." *Proc Amer Ant Soc,* ns, XV (1903), 385-444.

17 MAC GILL, Caroline E., et al. *History of Transportation in the United States before 1860.* New York, 1948.

18 MC KAY, Richard C. *South Street: A Maritime History of New York.* New York, 1934. (Useful, though anecdotal, and not always reliable.)

19 MESICK, Jane L. *The English Traveler in America, 1785-1835.* New York, 1922.

1 MILLS, James Cooke. *Our Inland Seas: Their Shipping and Commerce for Three Centuries.* Chicago, 1910.

2 NORTH, Douglass C. "Ocean Freight Rates and Economic Development, 1750-1913." *J Econ Hist,* XVIII (1958), 537-555.

3 PORTER, Kenneth W. *The Jacksons and the Lees: Two Generations of Massachusetts Merchants, 1765–1844. Stud Bus Hist* (Har). 2 vols. Cambridge, Mass., 1937.

4 RINGWALT, John L. *Development of Transportation Systems in the United States.* Philadelphia, 1888. Repr New York, 1966.

5 ROWE, William H. *The Maritime History of Maine: Three Centuries of Shipbuilding and Seafaring.* New York, 1948.

6 SHUMWAY, George. *Conestoga Wagon, 1750-1850 Freight Carrier for 100 Years of America's Westward Expansion.* 2d ed. York, Pa., 1966.

7 SPEARS, J. R. *The Story of the American Merchant Marine.* New York, 1910.

8 STEVEN, Margaret. *Merchant Campbell, 1769-1846: A Study in Colonial Trade.* New York, 1966.

9 THOMSON, T. R., comp. *Check List of Publications on American Railroads before 1841.* New York, 1942.

10 THWAITES, Reuben Gold, ed. *Early Western Travels, 1748-1846.* 32 vols. Cleveland, 1904-1907. (An important source for study of economic conditions in the Middle and Far West.)

11 United States Congress. *Report on the Internal Commerce of the United States.* House Executive Doc. No. 6, Pt. 2. 50th Cong., 1st Sess., 1888. Washington, D.C., 1888.

12 WAGNER, Henry R. *The Plains and the Rockies: A Bibliography of Original Narratives of Travel and Adventure, 1800-1865.* Rev ed. Columbus, 1953.

6. *Manufacturing, Industrial Organization, and Technology*

13 SCRIVENOR, Harry. *A Comprehensive History of the Iron Trade, Throughout the World.* London, 1841. (Chap xi on the U.S.)

* * * * * * *

14 BISHOP, J. L. *A History of American Manufactures, from 1608 to 1860.* 2 vols. Philadelphia, 1861-1864. Repr New York, 1966.

15 BOLLES, Albert S. *Industrial History of the United States.* Norwich, Conn., 1879. Repr New York, 1966.

16 CLARK, Victor S. *History of Manufactures in the United States, 1607-1860.* 3 vols. New York, 1929.

17 COLE, Arthur H. *The American Wool Manufacture.* 2 vols. Cambridge, Mass., 1926.

18 COYNE, F. E. *The Development of the Cooperage Industry in the United States, 1620-1940.* Chicago, 1940.

19 DERRY, T. K. and Trevor I. WILLIAMS. *A Short History of Technology from the Earliest Times to A.D. 1900.* New York, 1961.

GENERAL STUDIES

1 HAZARD, Blanch E. *The Organization of the Boot and Shoe Industry in Massachusetts before 1875. Har Econ Stud.* Cambridge, Mass., 1921,

2 HINDLE, Brooke. *Technology in Early America: Needs and Opportunities for Study with a Directory of Artifact Collections by Lucius F. Ellsworth.* Chapel Hill, 1966.†

3 KRANZBERG, Melvin and Carroll W. PURSELL, Jr., eds. *Technology in Western Civilization.* Vol I of *The Emergence of Modern Industrial Society Earlist Times to 1900.* New York, 1967.

4 KUHLMANN, Charles B. *The Development of the Flour-Milling Industry in the United States.* Boston, 1929.

5 MORRISON, John H. *History of New York Ship Yards.* New York, 1909.

6 OLIVER, John W. *History of American Technology.* New York, 1956.

7 PANSCHAR, William G. *Baking in America.* Vol. I of *Economic Development.* Evanston, Ill., 1958.

8 SCHMOOKLER, Jacob. *Invention and Economic Growth.* Cambridge, Mass., 1966.

9 SWANK, J. M. *The History of the Manufacture of Iron in all Ages.* 2d ed. Philadelphia, 1892. Repr New York, 1965.

10 SWANK, J. M. *Introduction to a History of Ironmaking and Coal Mining in Pennsylvania.* Philadelphia, 1878.

11 TRUMBULL, L. R. *A History of Industrial Paterson.* Paterson, N.J., 1882.

12 TRYON, R. M. *Household Manufactures in the United States, 1640-1860.* Chicago, 1917. Repr New York, 1966.

13 TUNNELL, James M., Jr. "The Manufacture of Iron in Sussex County." *Del Hist,* VI (1954), 85-91.

14 USHER, Abbott P. *A History of Mechanical Inventions.* Cambridge, Mass., 1954.†

15 WALKER, Joseph E. *Hopewell Village: A Social and Economic History of an Iron-Making Community.* Philadelphia, 1966.

16 WEEKS, Lyman H. *A History of Paper Manufacturing in the United States, 1690-1916.* New York, 1916.

17 WELSH, Peter C. *Tanning in the United States.* Washington, D.C., 1964.

18 WITTLINGER, Carlton T. "The Small Arms Industry of Lancaster County, 1710-1840." *Penn Hist,* XXIV (1957), 121-136.

7. Financial and Business Organization

19 ADAMS, Henry C. *Public Debts, an Essay in the Science of Finance.* New York, 1887. (A Standard, older study, now superseded.)

20 BENSON, George C. S., et al. *The American Property Tax: Its History, Administration, and Economic Impact.* Claremont, Calif., 1965.

21 BROOKS, Robert P. *The Financial History of Georgia, 1732–1950.* Athens, Ga., 1952.

GENERAL STUDIES

1. COLE, Arthur H. *Wholesale Commodity Prices in the United States, 1700-1861.* 2 vols. Cambridge, Mass., 1938.
2. DEWEY, Davis R. *Financial History of the United States.* 12th ed. New York, 1934.
3. EZELL, John. "The Rise and Decline of Lotteries in American History." Dissertation, Harvard Univ, 1947.
4. HAMMOND, Bray. *Banks and Politics in America, from the Revolution to the Civil War.* Princeton, 1957.†
5. HIDY, Ralph W. *The House of Baring in American Trade and Finance: English Merchant Bankers at Work, 1763-1861.* Stud Bus Hist (Har). Cambridge, Mass., 1949.
6. HOLDSWORTH, John T. *Financing an Empire: History of Banking in Pennsylvania.* 4 vols. Philadelphia, 1928.
7. HOLLANDER, J. H. *The Financial History of Baltimore.* Stud Hist Pol Sci (Hop). Baltimore, 1899.
8. MILLS, C. Wright. "The American Business Elite: A Collective Portrait." *J Econ Hist,* V (1945), 20-44.
9. RATNER, Sidney. *American Taxation: Its History as a Social Force in Democracy.* New York, 1942.
10. SHULTZ, W. J. and M. B. CAINE. *Financial Development of the United States.* New York, 1937.
11. SILBERLING, Norman J. *The Dynamics of Business.* New York, 1943.
12. STOKES, Howard K. *The Finances and Administration of Providence.* Baltimore, 1903.
13. STUDENSKI, Paul and Herman E. KROOSS. *Financial History of the United States.* New York, 1952.
14. SUMNER, William G. *A History of Banking in the U.S.* Vol. I. *A History of Banking in all the Leading Nations.* New York, 1896.
15. TAYLOR, George Rogers and Ethel D. HOOVER. *Employment, Growth and Price Levels.* See 9.11, 379-410. (Price indexes 1720-1958.)
16. WARREN, G. F., F.A. PEARSON, and H. M. STOKER. *Wholesale Prices for 213 years, 1720-1932.* Ithaca, 1932.
17. WHITE, Horace. *Money and Banking, Illustrated by American History.* 2d ed. Boston, 1902.

IV. The Colonial Period

1. General Studies

18. MAC PHERSON, David. *Annals of Commerce, Manufactures, Fisheries and Navigation.* 4 vols. Edinburgh, 1805.

* * * * * * *

19. ADAMS J. T. *Provincial Society, 1690-1763.* New York, 1927.
20. BILLINGTON, Ray A., ed. *The Reinterpretation of Early American History: Essays in Honor of John Edwin Pomfret.* San Marino, 1966.†

THE COLONIAL PERIOD

1 BRIDENBAUGH, Carl. *Cities in Revolt: Urban Life in America, 1743-1776.* New York, 1955.†
2 BRIDENBAUGH, Carl. *Cities in the Wilderness: The First Century of Urban Life in America, 1625-1742.* New York, 1938.†
3 CAREY, Lewis J. *Franklin's Economic Views.* New York, 1928.
4 DIAMOND, Sigmund. "Values as an Obstacle to Economic Growth: The American Colonies." *J Econ Hist,* XXVII (1967), 561-575.
5 DORFMAN, Joseph. "The Economic Philosophy of Thomas Paine." *Pol Sci Q,* LIII (1938), 372-386.
6 *Essays in Colonial History Presented to Charles McLean Andrews by His Students.* New Haven, 1931.
7 GIPSON, Lawrence H. *The British Empire before the American Revolution.* 13 vols. New York, 1936-1966.
8 GOODMAN, Paul. *Essays in American Colonial History.* New York, 1967.†
9 GREENE, E. B. *The Revolutionary Generation, 1763-1790.* New York, 1943.
10 JOHNSON, E. A. J. *American Economic Thought in the Seventeenth Century.* London, 1932. Repr New York, 1961.
11 LABAREE, Leonard W. *Conservatism in Early American History.* Ithaca, 1959.
12 LANDES, David. "Technological Change and Industrial Development in Western Europe, 1750-1914." *The Cambridge Economic History of Europe,* VI (1964), 274-585. (An excellent statement of the European background for American economic development.)
13 MORRIS, Richard B., ed. *The Era of the American Revolution.* New York, 1939.†
14 NETTELS, Curtis P. *The Roots of American Civilization: A History of American Colonial Life.* New York, 1938.†
15 SACHS, W. S. and Ari A. HOOGENBOOM. *The Enterprising Colonials: Society on the Eve of the Revolution.* Chicago, 1965.
16 SOUTHERLAND, Stella H. "Colonial Statistics." *Explo Entrep Hist,* 2d ser, V (1968), 58-107.
17 VER STEEG, Clarence L. *The Formative Years, 1607-1763.* New York, 1964.
18 VIRTUE, G. O. "Capitalistic Aspects of the Colonial Economy." *Explorations in Economics: Notes and Essays Contributed in Honor of F. W. Taussig.* New York, 1936, 507-515.
19 WERTENBAKER, T. J. *The First Americans, 1607-1690.* New York, 1927.
20 WRIGHT, Esmond. *Fabric of Freedom, 1763-1800.* New York, 1961.† (Good bibliography.)
21 WRIGHT, Louis B. *The Dream of Prosperity in Colonial America.* New York, 1965.
22 WRIGHT, Louis B. *New Interpretations of American Colonial History.* Washington, D.C., 1959.

2. Regional and Local Studies

1 ADAMS, J. T. *The Founding of New England.* Boston, 1921.†
2 ADAMS, J. T. *Revolutionary New England, 1691-1776.* Boston, 1923.
3 BREWSTER, William. *The Fourteen Commonwealths, Vermont and the States that Failed.* Philadelphia, 1960. (States that failed—Westmoreland, Franklin, and Transylvania.)
4 BRIDENBAUGH, Carl and Jessica. *Rebels and Gentlemen: Philadelphia in the Age of Franklin.* New York, 1942.†
5 BROWN, Richard M. *The South Carolina Regulators.* Cambridge, Mass., 1963.
6 BRUCE, P. A. *Economic History of Virginia in the Seventeenth Century.* 2 vols. New York, 1907.†
7 CARSON, Jane. *Travellers in Tidewater Virginia, 1700-1800.* Charlottesville, Va., 1965.†
8 CRANE, Verner W. *The Southern Frontier, 1670-1732.* Durham, N.C., 1928.
9 CRAVEN, W. F. *The Southern Colonies in the Seventeenth Century, 1607-1689.* Baton Rouge, 1949.
10 DAVIS, William T. *Professional and Industrial History of Suffolk County, Massachusetts.* 3 vols. Boston, 1894.
11 DAVISSON, William I. "Essex County Wealth Trends: Wealth and Economic Growth in Seventeenth Century Massachusetts." *Essex Inst Hist Coll,* CIII (1967), 291-342.
12 FEER, Robert A. "Imprisonment for Debt in Massachusetts before 1800." *Miss Val Hist Rev,* XLVIII (1961), 252-269.
13 GOULD, Clarence P. "Economic Causes of the Rise of Baltimore." See **17**.6, 225-251.
14 GRANT, Charles S. *Democracy in the Connecticut Frontier Town of Kent. Stud Hist Econ Pub Law* (Colum). New York, 1961.
15 GRISWOLD, A. Whitney. "Three Puritans on Prosperity." *N Eng Q,* VII (1934), 475-493. (Cotton Mather, Benjamin Franklin, and Timothy Dwight.)
16 HENRETTA, James A. "Economic Development and Social Structure in Colonial Boston." *Wm Mar Q,* 3d ser, XXII (1965), 75-92.
17 LABAREE, Benjamin and Edward M. Riley, with comments by Bayrd Still. "Local History Contributions and Techniques in the Study of Two Colonial Cities." *Bull Am Assn State Loc Hist.* Madison, 1959. (The two cities are Newburyport, Mass., and Williamsburg, Va.)
18 LAND, Aubrey C. "Economic Base and Social Structure: The Northern Chesapeake in the Eighteenth Century." *J Econ Hist,* XXV (1965), 639-654.
19 LAND, Aubrey C. "Economic Behavior in a Planting Society: The Eighteenth-Century Chesapeake." *J S Hist,* XXXIII (1967), 469-485.

1 LEMON, James T. "Urbanization and the Development of Eighteenth-Century Southeastern Pennsylvania and Adjacent Delaware." *Wm Mar Q*, 3d ser, XXIV (1967), 501-542.

2 LIPPINCOTT, Horace M. *Early Philadelphia, Its People, Life, and Progress.* Philadelphia, 1917.

3 MC KEE, Samuel, Jr. "The Economic Pattern of Colonial New York," in *History of the State of New York*. Ed. by Alexander C. Flick. New York, 1933, II, 247-282.

4 MERIWETHER, Robert L. *The Expansion of South Carolina, 1729-1765.* Kingsport, S.C., 1940.

5 MERRENS, H. R. *Colonial North Carolina in the Eighteenth Century: A Study in Historical Geography.* Chapel Hill, 1964.

6 MILLS, Robert. *Statistics of South Carolina, Including a View of Its Natural, Civil, and Military History, General and Particular.* Charleston, S.C., 1826.

7 MORISON, Samuel E. "The Plantation of Nashaway." *Pub Col Soc Mass*, XXVII (1927-1930), 204-222.

8 MORTON, Richard. *Colonial Virginia.* 2 vols. Chapel Hill, 1960.

9 PHILLIPS, James D. *Salem in the Seventeenth Century.* New York, 1933.

10 RUTMAN, Darrett B., ed. *The Old Dominion: Essays for Thomas Perkins Abernethy.* Charlottesville, Va., 1964.

11 SACHS, W. S. "The Business Outlook in the Northern Colonies, 1750-1775." Dissertation, Columbia Univ, 1957.

12 SELLERS, Leila. *Charleston Business on the Eve of the American Revolution.* Chapel Hill, 1934.

13 SOLTOW, James H. *The Economic Role of Williamsburg.* Charlottesville, Va., 1965.†

14 SYRETT, Harold C. "Private Enterprise in New Amsterdam." *Wm Mar Q*, 3d ser, XI (1954), 536-550.

15 WEEDEN, W. B. *Economic and Social History of New England, 1620-1789.* 2 vols. Boston, 1890.

16 WELSH, Peter C. "Merchants, Millers, and Ocean ships: The Components of an Early American Industrial Town." *Del Hist*, VII (1957), 319-336. (The town is Wilmington.)

17 WERTENBAKER, T. J. *Norfolk: Historic Southern Port.* 2d ed. Durham, N.C., 1962.

18 WERTENBAKER, T. J. *Patrician and Plebeian in Virginia or the Origin and Development of the Social Classes of the Old Dominion.* Charlottesville, Va., 1910. Repr New York, 1959.

19 ZERCHNER, Oscar. *Connecticut's Years of Controversy, 1750-1776.* Chapel Hill, 1949.

3. *Population, Immigration, and the Migration Westward*

20 BOLTON, Ethel S. "Immigrants to New England, 1700-1775." *Essex Inst Hist Coll*, LXVII (1931), 89-112, 201-224, 305-328.

1. BREWSTER, William. *The Pennsylvania and New York Frontier, History of from 1720 to the Close of the Revolution.* Philadelphia, 1954.

2. BUCK, Solon J. and E. H. *The Planting of Civilization in Western Pennsylvania.* Cambridge, Mass., 1941.

3. CARUSO, John A. *The Appalachian Frontier: America's First Surge Westward.* Indianapolis, 1959.

4. DUNAWAY, Wayland F. *The Scotch-Irish of Colonial Pennsylvania.* Chapel Hill, 1944.

5. FRENCH, Allen. *Charles I and the Puritan Upheaval: A Study of the Causes of the Great Migration.* Boston, 1955.

6. GRAHAM, Ian C. C. *Colonists from Scotland: Emigration to North America, 1707-1783.* Ithaca, 1956.

7. GREENE, E. B. and V. D. HARRINGTON. *American Population before the Federal Census of 1790.* New York, 1932. Repr New York, 1967.

8. HAVIGHURST, Walter. *Wilderness for Sale: The Story of the First Western Land Rush.* New York, 1956.

9. LEACH, Douglas E. *The Northern Colonial Frontier, 1607-1763.* New York, 1966.

10. LOCKRIDGE, Kenneth A. "The Population of Dedham, Massachusetts, 1636-1736." *Econ Hist Rev,* 2d ser, XIX (1966), 318-344.

11. MEYER, Duane. *The Highland Scots of North Carolina, 1732-1776.* Chapel Hill, 1961.

12. SHIPTON, Clifford K. "Immigration to New England, 1680-1740." *J Pol Econ,* XLIV (1936), 225-239.

13. SMITH, Abbot E. "The Transportation of Convicts to the American Colonies in the Seventeenth Century." *Am Hist Rev,* XXXIX (1934), 232-249.

14. SUTHERLAND, Stella H. *Population Distribution in Colonial America.* New York, 1936.

15. TAYLOR, Paul S. "Colonizing Georgia, 1732-1752: A Statistical Note." *Wm Mar Q,* 3d ser, XXII (1965), 119-127.

4. Agriculture and Land Ownership

16. *American Husbandry, Containing an Account of the Soil, Climate, Production, and Agriculture of the British Colonies in North America and the West Indies.* 2 vols. London, 1775.

17. "The Case of the Planters of Tobacco in Virginia, & C." London, 1733. Repr in 7.16.

* * * * * * *

18. BALLAGH, James C. *Introduction to Southern Economic History—The Land System. Am Hist Assn, Ann Rep for 1897.* Washington, D.C., 1898, 99-129.

19. BARNES, Viola F. "Land Tenure in English Colonial Charters of the Seventeenth Century." See **17.6**, 4-40.

20. BENNETT, M. K. "The Food Economy of the New England Indians, 1605-1675." *J Pol Econ,* LXII (1955), 369-397.

THE COLONIAL PERIOD

1 BOND, Beverley W. *The Quit-Rent System in the American Colonies.* New Haven, 1919.

2 CARRIER, Lyman. *The Beginnings of Agriculture in America.* New York, 1923.

3 CRAVEN, Avery O. *Soil Exhaustion as a Factor in the Agricultural History of Virginia and Maryland, 1606-1860. Stud Soc Sci* (Ill.) Urbana, 1925.

4 GAGLIARDO, John G. "Germans and Agriculture in Colonial Pennsylvania." *Penn Mag Hist Biog,* LXXXIII (1959), 192-218.

5 GIPSON, Lawrence H. "Virginia Planter Debts before the American Revolution." *Va Mag Hist Biog,* LXIX (1961), 259-277.

6 HARLEY, R. Bruce. "Dr. Charles Carroll—Land Speculator, 1730-1755." *Md Hist Mag,* XLVI (1951), 93-107.

7 HARRIS, Marshall. *Origin of the Land Tenure System in the United States.* Ames, Iowa, 1953.

8 HAYWOOD, C. Robert. "Mercantilism and South Carolina Agriculture, 1700-1763." *S C Hist Mag,* LX (1959), 15-27.

9 LEMON, James T. "Household Consumption in Eighteenth-Century America and its Relationship to Production and Trade: The Situation among Farmers in Southeastern Pennsylvania." *Ag Hist,* XLI (1967), 59-70.

10 MARK, Irving. *Agrarian Conflicts in the Colony of New York.* New York, 1940.

11 MINGAY, G. E. "The Agricultural Depression, 1730-1750." *Econ Hist Rev,* 2d ser, VIII (1956), 323-338.

12 OLSON, A. L. *Agricultural Economy and the Population in Eighteenth-Century Connecticut.* Tercentenary Commission of the State of Connecticut. New Haven, 1935.

13 SACHS, W. S. "Agricultural Conditions in the Northern Colonies before the Revolution." *J Econ Hist,* XIII (1953), 274-290.

14 SALOUTOS, Theodore. "Efforts at Crop Control in Seventeenth Century America." *J S Hist,* XII (1946), 45-66.

15 SCOVILLE, Warren C. "Did Colonial Farmers 'Waste' Our Land?" *S Econ J,* XX (1953), 178-181.

16 SHRYOCK, Richard. "British Versus German Traditions in Colonial Agriculture." *Miss Val Hist Rev,* XXVI (1939), 39-54.

17 SIOUSSAT, St. George L. "The Breakdown of the Royal Management of Lands in the Southern Provinces, 1773-1775." *Ag Hist,* III (1929), 67-98.

18 WERTENBAKER, T. J. *The Planters of Colonial Virginia.* Princeton, 1922.

5. Extractive Industry Other than Agriculture

19 HARTLEY, E. N. *Ironworks on the Saugus: The Lynn and Braintree Ventures of the Company of Undertakers of the Ironworks in New England.* Norman, Okla., 1957.

1. INNIS, Harold A. "Interrelations between the Fur Trade of Canada and the United States." *Miss Val Hist Rev,* XX (1933), 321-332.
2. JACOBS, Wilbur R. "Unsavory Sidelights on the Colonial Fur Trade." *N Y Hist,* XXXIV (1953), 135-148.
3. JUDAH, Charles B., Jr. *The North American Fisheries and British Policy to 1713.* Urbana, 1933.
4. LAWSON, M. G. *Fur: A Study in English Mercantilism, 1700-1775.* Toronto, 1943.
5. MALONE, Joseph J. *Pine Trees and Politics: The Naval Stores and Forest Policy in Colonial New England, 1691-1775.* Seattle, 1964.
6. MOLONEY, Francis X. *The Fur Trade in New England, 1620-1676.* Cambridge, Mass., 1931.
7. NASH, Gary B. "The Quest for the Susquehanna Valley: New York, Pennsylvania, and the Seventeenth-Century Fur Trade." *N Y Hist,* XLVIII (1967), 3-27.
8. RANSOM, James M. *Vanishing Ironworks of the Ramapos: The Story of the Forges, Furnaces, and Mines of the New Jersey—New York Border Area.* New Brunswick, 1966.
9. STEVENS, Wayne E. *The Northwest Fur-Trade, 1763-1800.* Stud Soc Sci (Ill). Urbana, 1928.
10. THEISS, Lewis E. "Lumbering in Penn's Woods." *Penn Hist,* XIX (1952), 397-412.

6. Transportation

11. CATLIN, George B. "Early Travel on the Ohio and Its Tributaries." *Md Hist Mag,* XX (1936), 153-161.
12. CRITTENDEN, C. C. "Overland Travel and Transportation in North Carolina, 1763-1789." *N C Hist Rev,* VIII (1931), 239-257.
13. GOULD, Clarence P. *Money and Transportation in Maryland, 1720-1765.* Stud Hist Pol Sci (Hop). Baltimore, 1915.
14. JONES, Herbert G. *The King's Highway from Portland to Kittery: Stagecoach and Tavern Days on the Old Post Road.* Freeport, Me., 1953.
15. KINCAID, Robert L. *The Wilderness Road.* New York, 1947.
16. MC CUSKER, John J. "Colonial Tonnage Measurement: Five Philadelphia Merchant Ships as a Sample." *J Econ Hist,* XXVII (1967), 82-91.
17. MITCHELL, Isabel S. *Roads and Road-Making in Colonial Connecticut.* Tercentenary Commission of the State of Connecticut. New Haven, 1933.
18. OMWAKE, John. *The Conestoga Six-Horse Bell Teams of Eastern Pennsylvania.* Cincinnati, 1930.
19. PHELPS, Dawson A. "Travel on the Natchez Trace." *J Miss Hist,* XV (1953), 155-164.
20. VERHOEFF, Mary. *The Kentucky Mountains, Transportation and Commerce, 1750-1911: A Study in the Economic History of a Coal Field.* Louisville, 1911.

1 WALTON, Gary M. "Colonial Tonnage Measurements: A Comment." *J Econ Hist,* XXVII (1967), 392-397.

2 WALTON, Gary M. "New Evidence on Colonial Commerce." *J Econ Hist,* XXVIII (1968), 363-389.

3 WALTON, Gary M. "Sources of Productivity Change in American Colonial Shipping, 1675-1775." *Econ Hist Rev,* 2d ser, XX (1967), 67-78.

7. *Commerce*

A. THE MERCHANTS

4 WHITE, Philip L., ed. *The Beekman Mercantile Papers, 1747-1799.* 3 vols. New York, 1956.

* * * * * * *

5 BAILYN, Bernard. *The New England Merchants in the Seventeenth Century.* Cambridge, Mass., 1955.†

6 BAXTER, W. T. *The House of Hancock: Business in Boston, 1724-1775.* Stud Bus Hist (Har). Cambridge, Mass., 1945.

7 BIGELOW, Bruce M. "Aaron Lopez: Merchant of Newport." *N Eng Q,* IV (1931), 757-776.

8 BROSHAR, Helen. "The First Push Westward of the Albany Traders." *Miss Val Hist Rev,* VII (1920), 228-241.

9 BRUCHEY, Stuart. *The Colonial Merchant: Sources and Readings.* New York, 1966.†

10 COLE, Arthur H. "The Tempo of Mercantile Life in Colonial America." *Bus Hist Rev,* XXXIII (1959), 277-299.

11 DAVIES, K. G. "The Origins of the Commission System in the West India Trade." *Tran Royal Hist Soc,* 5th ser, II (1952), 89-107.

12 DAVISON, Robert A. *Isaac Hicks: New York Merchant and Quaker, 1767-1820.* Stud Bus Hist (Har). Cambridge, Mass., 1964.

13 DOUDS, Howard C. "Merchants and Merchandising in Pittsburgh, 1759-1800." *W Penn Hist Mag,* XX (1937), 123-132.

14 EAST, Robert A. "The Business Entrepreneurs in a Changing Colonial Economy, 1763-1795." *J Econ Hist,* VI (1946), 16-27.

15 EDELMAN, Edward. "Thomas Hancock, Colonial Merchant." *J Econ Bus Hist,* I (1928), 77-104.

16 EVANS, Emory G. "The Rise and Decline of the Virginia Aristocracy in the Eighteenth Century: The Nelsons." See **19**.10, 62-78.

17 FAIRCHILD, Bryon. *Messrs. William Pepperell: Merchants at Piscataqua.* Ithaca, 1954.

18 HARRINGTON, V. D. *The New York Merchant on the Eve of the Revolution.* Stud Hist Econ Pub Law (Colum). New York, 1935.

19 HEDGES, James B. *The Browns of Providence Plantation: Colonial Years.* Cambridge, Mass., 1952.

20 JOHNSON, Victor L. "Fair Traders and Smugglers in Philadelphia, 1754-1763." *Penn Mag Hist Biog,* LXXXIII (1959), 125-149.

1. LABAREE, Benjamin. *Patriots and Patricians: The Merchants of Newburyport, 1764-1815.* Har Hist Stud. Cambridge, Mass., 1962.
2. MALONE, M. S. "Falmouth and the Shenandoah: Trade before the Revolution." *Am Hist Rev,* XL (1935), 693-703.
3. MARTIN, Margaret E. *Merchants and Trade of the Connecticut River Valley, 1750-1820.* Stud Hist (Smith). Northampton, Mass., 1939
4. PHILLIPS, James D. "The Life and Times of Richard Derby, Merchant of Salem." *Essex Inst Hist Coll,* LV (1929), 243-289.
5. ROBERTS, William I., III. "Samuel Storke: An Eighteenth-Century London Merchant Trading to the American Colonies." *Bus Hist Rev,* XXXIX (1965), 147-170.
6. SCHLESINGER, Arthur M. *The Colonial Merchants and the American Revolution, 1763-1776.* Stud Hist Econ Pub Law (Colum). New York, 1918.
7. SOLTOW, James H. "Scottish Traders in Virginia, 1750-1775." *Econ Hist Rev,* 2d ser, XII (1959), 83-99.
8. TAPLEY, Harriet S. "Richard Skinner, an Early Eighteenth-Century Merchant of MarbleHead." *Essex Inst Hist Coll,* LXVIII (1942), 5-29.
9. THOMSON, Robert P. "The Merchant in Virginia, 1700-1775." Dissertation, U. of Wis., 1955.
10. TOLLES, Frederick B. *Meeting House and Counting House: The Quaker Merchants of Colonial Philadelphia, 1682-1763.* New York, 1963.†
11. WEAVER, Glenn. *Jonathan Trumbull: Connecticut's Merchant Magistrate (1710-1785).* Cambridge, Mass., 1952.
12. WHITE, Philip L. *The Beekmans of New York in Politics and Commerce, 1647-1877.* New York, 1956.

B. TRADE

13. BABSON, David L. "Maritime History of Gloucester, 1600-1807." Unpub Washburn Prize Essay, Harvard Univ, 1932.
14. BRISSOT, J. P. *The Commerce of America with Europe: Particularly with France and Great Britain.* New York, 1795.
15. DONNAN, Elizabeth, ed. *Documents Illustrative of the History of the Slave Trade to America.* 4 vols. Washington, D.C., 1931-1935.
16. MAC MASTER, Richard K. and David C. SKAGGS, eds. "The Letterbooks of Alexander Hamilton, Piscataway Factor." *Md Hist Mag,* LXI (1966), 146-166, 305-328; LXII (1967), 135-169.
17. *Report of a Committee of the Lords of the Privy Council on the Trade of Great Britain with the United States, Jan. 1791.* Washington, D.C., 1888.
18. WHITWORTH, Charles. *State of the Trade of Great Britain in Its Imports and Exports Progressively from the Year 1697.* London, 1776.

* * * * * * *

19. ANDREWS, Charles M. "Colonial Commerce." *Am Hist Rev,* XX (1914), 43-63.

1 BAILYN, Bernard. "Communications and Trade: The Atlantic in the Seventeenth Century." *J Econ Hist,* XIII (1953), 378-387.

2 BAILYN, Bernard and Lotte. *Massachusetts Shipping, 1697-1714: A Statistical Study.* Cambridge, Mass., 1959.

3 BARKER, T. C. "Smuggling in the Eighteenth Century: The Evidence of the Sottish Tobacco Trade." *Va Mag Hist Biog,* LXII (1954), 387-399.

4 BELL, Herbert C. "The West India Trade before the American Revolution." *Am Hist Rev,* XXII (1916), 272-287.

5 BOWDEN, William H. "The Commerce of Marblehead, 1665-1775." *Essex Inst Hist Coll,* LXVIII (1931), 117-146.

6 CLOWSE, Converse D. "The Charleston Export Trade, 1717-1737." Dissertation, Northwestern U, 1963.

7 COLE, W. A. "Trends in Eighteenth-Century Smuggling." *Econ Hist Rev,* 2d ser, X (1958), 395-410.

8 CRAWFORD, Walter F. "Commerce of Rhode Island with the Southern and Continental Colonies in the Eighteenth Century." *Proc R I Hist Soc,* XIV (1921), 99-110, 124-130.

9 CRITTENDEN, C. C. *The Commerce of North Carolina, 1763-1789.* New Haven, 1936.

10 DONNAN, Elizabeth. "The Slave Trade into South Carolina before the Revolution." *Am Hist Rev,* XXXIII (1928), 804-823.

11 DOW, George F. "Shipping and Trade in Early New England." *Proc Mass Hist Soc,* LXIV (1930), 185-201.

12 "Early Coastwise and Foreign Shipping of Salem." *Essex Inst Hist Coll,* LXVII (1931), 49-64, 241-256, 337-352.

13 GIDDENS, Paul H. "Trade and Industry in Colonial Maryland, 1753-1769." *J Econ Bus Hist,* IV (1932), 512-538.

14 GILLINGHAM, Harold E. *Marine Insurance in Philadelphia, 1721-1800.* Philadelphia, 1933.

15 GOEBEL, Dorothy B. "The 'New England Trade' and the French West Indies, 1763-1774: A Study in Trade Policies." *Wm Mar Q,* 3d ser, XX (1963), 331-372.

16 HANNA, Mary A. *The Trade of the Delaware District before the Revolution. Stud Hist* (Smith). Northampton, Mass., 1917.

17 HEMPHILL, John, II. "Freight Rates in the Maryland Tobacco Trade, 1705-1762." *Md Hist Mag,* LIV (1959), 36-60, 153-187.

18 HOOGENBOOM, Ari A. "The Commerce of Boston, 1752-1765." Master's Thesis, Columbia Univ, 1951.

19 HOOKER, Roland M. *The Colonial Trade of Connecticut.* Publications of the Tercentenary Commission of the State of Connecticut. New Haven, 1936.

20 HUGHSON, Shirley C. *The Carolina Pirates and Colonial Commerce, 1670-1740. Stud Hist Pol Sci* (Hop). Baltimore, 1894.

21 JAMESON, John F., ed. *Privateering and Piracy in the Colonial Period.* New York, 1923.

1 JENSEN, Arthur L. *The Maritime Commerce of Colonial Philadelphia.* Madison, 1963.

2 LANIER, Mary J. "The Earlier Development of Boston as a Commercial Centre." Dissertation, Univ of Chicago, 1924.

3 LYDON, James G. "Fish and Flour for Gold: Southern Europe and the Colonial American Balance of Payments." *Bus Hist Rev,* XXXIX (1965), 171-183.

4 LYDON, James G. "Philadelphia's Commercial Expansion, 1720-1739." *Penn Mag Hist Biog,* XCI (1967), 401-418.

5 MAKINSON, David H. *Barbados: A Study of North-American–West Indian Relations, 1739-1789.* The Hague, 1964.

6 MIDDLETON, Arthur P. *Tobacco Coast: A Maritime History of Chesapeake Bay in the Colonial Era.* Newport News, 1953.

7 MORRISS, M. S. *Colonial Trade of Maryland, 1689-1715. Stud Hist Pol Sci* (Hop). Baltimore, 1914.

8 NETTELS, Curtis P. "The Economic Relations of Boston, Philadelphia, and New York, 1680-1715." *J Econ Bus Hist,* III (1930), 185-215.

9 OSTRANDER, Gilman M. "The Colonial Molasses Trade." *Ag Hist,* XXX (1956), 77-84.

10 PARES, Richard. *Yankees and Creoles: The Trade between North America and the West Indies before the American Revolution.* Cambridge, Mass., 1956.

11 PRICE, Jacob M. "The Economic Growth of the Chesapeake and the Economic Market, 1697-1775." *J Econ Hist,* XXIV (1964), 496-511.

12 PRICE, Jacob M. "The Rise of Glasgow in the Chesapeake Tobacco Trade, 1707–1775." *Wm Mar Q,* 3d ser, XI (1954), 179-199.

13 ROSENBLATT, Samuel M. "The Significance of Credit in the Tobacco Consignment Trade: A Study of John Norton & Sons, 1768-1775." *Wm Mar Q,* 3d ser, XIX (1962), 383–399.

14 SALTONSTALL, William G. *Ports of Piscataqua.* Cambridge, Mass., 1941.

15 SHEPARD, James. "A Balance of Payments for the Thirteen Colonies, 1768-1772." Dissertation, Univ of Washington, 1965. (A summary appears in *J Econ Hist,* XXV (1965), 691-695.)

16 SURREY, N. M. M. *The Commerce of Louisiana during the French Regime, 1699-1763. Stud Hist Econ Pub Law* (Colum). New York, 1916.

17 THOMSON, Robert P. "The Tobacco Export of the Upper James River Naval District, 1773-1775." *Wm Mar Q,* 3d ser, XVIII (1961), 393-401.

18 WALTON, Gary M. "A Quantitative Study of American Colonial Shipping." Dissertation, Univ of Washington, 1966.

8. Industry

19 BAGNALL, William R. *The Textile Industries of the U.S., 1639-1810.* Cambridge, Mass., 1893.

20 BINING, Arthur C. *Pennsylvania Iron Manufacture in the Eighteenth Century.* Harrisburg, 1938.

1 BRIDENBAUGH, Carl. *The Colonial Craftsman.* New York, 1950.†
2 CHAPMAN, Leonard B. "The Mast Industry of Old Falmouth." *Me Hist Soc Coll,* 2d ser, VII (1896), 390-403.
3 FELDMAN, Egal. "New York's Men's Clothing Trade, 1800-1861." Dissertation, Univ of Penn., 1959.
4 HUNTER, Dard. *Papermaking in Pioneer America.* Philadelphia, 1952.
5 JOHNSON, Keach. "The Genesis of the Baltimore Ironworks [1718-1737]." *J S Hist,* XIX (1953), 157-179.
6 LORD, Eleanor L. *Industrial Experiments in the British Colonies of North America.* Baltimore, 1898.
7 NETTELS, Curtis P. "The Menace of Colonial Manufacturing, 1690-1720." *N Eng Q,* IV (1931), 230-269.
8 NEU, Irene D. "The Iron Plantations of Colonial New York." *N Y Hist,* XXXIII (1952), 3-24.
9 PARKER, P. "The Philadelphia Printer: A Study of an Eighteenth Century Businessman." *Bus Hist Rev,* XL (1966), 24-46.
10 PEASE, George B. "Timothy Palmer, Bridge-Builder of the Eighteenth Century." *Essex Inst Hist Coll,* LXXXIII (1947), 97-111.
11 TUSTIN, E. B., Jr. "The Story of Salt in New England." *Essex Inst Hist Coll,* LXXXV (1949), 259-271.
12 VAN WAGENEN, Jared. *The Golden Age of Homespun.* Ithaca, 1953.†
13 WEAVER, Glenn. "Industry in an Agrarian Economy: Early Eighteenth Century Connecticut." *Conn Hist Soc Bull,* XIX (1954), 82-92.

9. Labor

14 BALLAGH, James C. *White Servitude in the Colony of Virginia.* Baltimore, 1895. Repr New York, 1967.
15 CLARK, Dora Mae. "The Impressment of Seamen in the American Colonies." See **17.6**, 198-224.
16 DYER, Walter A. *Early American Craftsmen.* New York, 1915.
17 FORBES, Allan W. "Apprenticeship in Massachusetts: Its Early Importance and Later Neglect." *Worcester Hist Soc Pub,* II (1936), 4-25.
18 GEISER, K. F. *Redemptioners and Indetured Servants in the Colony and Commonwealth of Pennsylvania.* New Haven, 1901.
19 HANDLIN, Oscar and Mary. "Origins of the Southern Labor System." *Wm Mar Q,* 3d ser, VII (1950), 199-222.
20 HAYWOOD, C. Robert. "Mercantilism and Colonial Slave Labor, 1700-1763." *J S Hist,* XXIII (1957), 454-464.
21 HOHMAN, Elmo P. *History of American Merchant Seamen.* Hamden, Conn., 1956.
22 JERNEGAN, Marcus W. *Laboring and Dependent Classes in Colonial America, 1607-1783.* Chicago, 1931. Repr New York, 1960.
23 JORDAN, Winthrop D. "Modern Tensions and the Origins of American Slavery." *J S Hist,* XXVIII (1962), 18-30.

THE COLONIAL PERIOD

1. MC ANEAR, Beverly. "The Place of the Freeman in Old New York." *N Y Hist,* XXI (1940), 418-430.
2. MC KEE, Samuel, Jr. *Labor in Colonial New York, 1664-1776. Stud Hist Econ Pub Law* (Colum). New York, 1935.
3. MORRIS, Richard B. *Government and Labor in Early America.* New York, 1946.†
4. MORRIS, Richard B. "Labor and Mercantilism in the Revolutionary Era." See 17.13, 76-139.
5. SMITH, Abbot E. *Colonists in Bondage: White Servitude and Convict Labor in America, 1607-1776.* Chapel Hill, 1947.
6. SMITH, Abbot E. "Indentured Servants: New Light on Some of America's 'First' Families." *J Econ Hist,* II (1942), 40-53.
7. SPEARS, J. R. *The American Slave Trade: An Account of its Origin, Growth, and Suppression.* New York, 1901.
8. SPRUILL, Julia C. *Women's Life and Work in the Southern Colonies.* Chapel Hill, 1938.

10. Financial Organization

9. DAVIS, Andrew M. *Colonial Currency Reprints.* 4 vols. Boston, 1910-1911. Repr New York, 1964.
10. DOUGLASS, William. *A Discourse Concerning the Currencies of the British Plantations in America.* Boston, 1740.
11. FELT, Joseph B. *An Historical Account of Massachusetts Currency.* Boston, 1839.

* * * * * *

12. BELZ, Herman J. "Currency Reform in Colonial Massachusetts, 1749-1750." *Essex Inst Hist Coll,* CIII (1967), 66-84.
13. BEZANSON, Anne, et al. *Prices in Colonial Pennsylvania.* Philadelphia, 1935.
14. BILLIAS, George A. *The Massachusetts Land Bankers of 1740. Stud* (Me). Orono, Me., 1959.
15. BRONSON, Henry. "A Historical Account of Connecticut Currency, Continental Money, and the Finances of the Revolution." *Pap New Haven Colony Hist Soc,* I (1865), 1-192.
16. BULLOCK, Charles J. *Essays on the Monetary History of the United States.* New York, 1900.

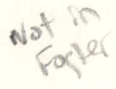

17. BURSTEIN, M. L. "Colonial Currency and Contemporary Monetary Theory: A Review Article." *Explo Entrep Hist,* 2d ser, III (1966), 220-233.
18. COLE, Arthur H. "Evolution of the Foreign-Exchange Markets of the United States." *J Econ Bus Hist,* I (1929), 386-421.
19. COLEMAN, Peter J. "The Insolvent Debtor in Rhode Island, 1745-1828." *Wm Mar Q,* 3d ser, XXII (1965), 413-434.
20. CRANDALL, Ruth. "Wholesale Commodity Prices in Boston During the Eighteenth Century." *Rev Econ Stat,* XVI (1934), 117-135.

THE COLONIAL PERIOD

1 DAVIS, Andrew M. *Currency and Banking in the Province of the Massachusetts-Bay.* 2 vols. New York, 1901.

2 DAVISSON, William I. "Essex County Price Trends: Money and Markets in Seventeenth Century Massachusetts." *Essex Inst Hist Coll,* CIII (1967), 144-185.

3 ELLERTSEN, E. Peter. "Prosperity and Paper Money: The Loan Office Act of 1723." *N J Hist,* LXXXV (1967), 47-57.

4 ERNEST, Joseph A. "Genesis of the Currency Act of 1764: Virginia Paper Money and the Protection of British Investments." *Wm Mar Q,* 3d ser, XXII (1965), 33-74.

5 EZELL, John. "The Lottery in Colonial America." *Wm Mar Q,* 3d ser, V (1948), 185-200.

6 FERGUSON, E. James. "Currency Finance: An Interpretation of Colonial Monetary Practices." *Wm Mar Q,* 3d ser, X (1953), 153-180.

7 GIPSON, Lawrence H. "The Taxation of the Connecticut Towns, 1750-1775." See **17**.16, 284-298.

8 GOULD, Clarence P. *Money and Transportation in Maryland, 1720-1765.* See **22**.13.

9 GREENE, Jack P. and Richard M. JELLISON. "The Currency Act of 1764 in Imperial-Colonial Relations, 1764-1776." *Wm Mar Q,* 3d ser, XVIII (1961), 485-518.

10 HICKCOX, John H. *A History of the Bills of Credit or Paper Money Issued by New York from 1709 to 1789.* Albany, 1866.

11 JELLISON, Richard M. "Paper Currency in Colonial South Carolina: A Reappraisal." *S C Hist Mag,* LXII (1961), 134-148.

12 JOHNSON, R. C. "Lotteries of the Virginia Company, 1612-1621." *Va Mag Hist Biog,* LXXIV (1966), 259-292.

13 KEMMERER, Donald L. "A History of Paper Money in Colonial New Jersey, 1668-1775." *Proc N J Hist Soc,* LXXIV (1956), 107-144.

14 LESTER, Richard A. *Monetary Experiments, Early American and Recent Scandinavian.* Princeton, 1939.

15 NETTELS, Curtis P. "British Payments in the American Colonies, 1685-1715." *Eng Hist Rev,* XLVIII (1933), 229-249.

16 NETTELS, Curtis P. "British Policy and Colonial Money Supply." *Econ Hist Rev,* III (1931), 219-245.

17 NETTELS, Curtis P. *The Money Supply of the American Colonies before 1720.* Stud Soc Sci Hist (Wis), Madison, 1934.

18 NORTON, William B. "Paper Currency in Massachusetts during the Revolution." *N Eng Q,* VII (1934), 43-69.

19 PHILLIPS, Henry. *Historical Sketches of the Paper Currency of the American Colonies, Prior to the Adoption of the Federal Constitution.* 2 vols. Roxbury, Mass., 1865-1866.

20 RIPLEY, William Z. *The Financial History of Virginia, 1609-1776.* New York, 1893.

21 SCOTT, Kenneth. *Counterfeiting in Colonial America.* New York, 1957.

22 SHERIDAN, Richard B. "The British Credit Crises of 1772 and the American Colonies." *J Econ Hist,* XX (1960), 161-186.

1 TAYLOR, George Rogers. "Wholesale Commodity Prices at Charleston, South Carolina, 1732-1791." *J Econ Bus Hist,* IV (1932), 356-377.
2 THAYER, Theodore G. "The Land Bank System in the American Colonies." *J Econ Hist,* XIII (1953), 145-159.
3 WAINWRIGHT, Nicholas B. *A Philadelphia Story: The Philadelphia Contributionship for the Insurance of Houses from Loss by Fire.* Philadelphia, 1952.

11. *Governmental Relationships*

A. PROMOTION AND REGULATION OF ECONOMIC DEVELOPMENT

4 ANDREWS, Charles M. *England's Commercial and Colonial Policy.* Vol IV of *The Colonial Period of American History.* New Haven, 1938.
5 ASHLEY, M. P. *Financial and Commercial Policy Under the Cromwellian Protectorate.* 2d rev ed. New York, 1962.
6 BARROW, Thomas C. *Trade and Empire: The British Customs Service in Colonial America, 1660-1775.* Cambridge, Mass., 1967.
7 BEER, George L. *British Colonial Policy, 1754-1765.* New York, 1907. Repr New York, 1922.
8 BEER, George L. *The Old Colonial System, 1660-1754.* 2 vols. New York, 1912.
9 BEER, George L. *Origins of the British Colonial System, 1578-1660.* New York, 1908. Repr New York, 1933.
10 BINING, Arthur C. *British Regulation of the Colonial Iron Industry.* Philadelphia, 1933.
11 DICKERSON, O. M. "The Attempt to Extend British Customs Controls over Intercolonial Commerce by Land." *S Atl Q,* L (1951), 361-368.
12 GIESECKE, Albert A. *American Commercial Legislation before 1789.* New York, 1910.
13 HALLER, William. *The Puritan Frontier: Town-Planning in New England: Colonial Development. 1630-1660.* New York, 1951.
14 HARPER, Lawrence A. "The Effect of the Navigation Acts on the Thirteen Colonies." See **17.13**, 3-39.
15 HARPER, Lawrence A. *The English Navigation Laws.* New York, 1939.
16 HEMPHILL, John, II. "Virginia and the English Commercial System, 1689-1733." Dissertation, Princeton U, 1964.
17 JENSEN, Arthur L. "The Inspection of Exports in Colonial Pennsylvania." *Penn Mag Hist Biog,* LXXVIII (1954), 275-297.
18 JONES, Newton B. "Weights, Measures, and Mercantilism: The Inspection of Exports in Virginia, 1742-1820." See **19.10**, 122-134.
19 KOHLMEIER, Albert L. "The Adequacy of the Imperialist View of Colonial History." *Ind Mag Hist,* XLV (1949), 113-122.
20 MARTIN, Alfred S. "The King's Customs: Philadelphia, 1763-1774." *Wm Mar Q,* 3d ser, V (1948), 201-216.

1. NETTELS, Curtis P. "British Mercantilism and the Economic Development of the Thirteen Colonies." *J Econ Hist,* XII (1952), 105-114.
2. NETTELS, Curtis P. "The Place of Markets in the Old Colonial System." *N Eng Q,* VI (1933), 491-512.
3. SELLERS, Charles G., Jr. "Private Profits and British Colonial Policy: The Speculations of Henry Mc Culloch." *Wm Mar Q,* 3d ser, VIII (1951), 535-551.
4. SETSER, Vernon G. *The Commercial Reciprocity Policy of the United States, 1774-1829.* Philadelphia, 1937.
5. SHERIDAN, Richard B. "The Molasses Act and the Market Strategy of the British Sugar Planters." *J Econ Hist,* XVII (1957), 62-83.
6. SOSIN, Jack M. *Whitehall and the Wilderness: The Middle West in British Colonial Policy, 1760-1775.* Lincoln, Neb., 1961.
7. THOMAS, Robert P. "A Quantitative Approach to the Study of the Effects of British Imperial Policy upon Colonial Welfare: Some Preliminary Findings." *J Econ Hist,* XXV (1965), 615-638.
8. UBBELOHDE, Carl. *The Vice-Admiralty Courts and the American Revolution.* Chapel Hill, 1960.
9. WIENER, Federick B. "The Rhode Island Merchants and the Sugar Act." *N Eng Q,* III (1930), 464-500.
10. WILLIAMS, William A. "The Age of Mercantilism: An Interpretation of the American Political Economy, 1763-1828." *Wm Mar Q,* 3d ser, XV (1958), 419-437.
11. WYCKOFF, Vertrees J. *Tobacco Regulation in Colonial Maryland.* Stud Hist Pol Sci (Hop). Baltimore, 1936.

B. ECONOMIC FACTORS IN POLITICAL DEVELOPMENT

12. ABERNETHY, T. P. *Western Lands and the American Revolution.* New York, 1937.
13. ANDREWS, Charles M. "Boston Merchants and the Non-Importation Movement." *Pub Colo Soc Mass,* XIX (1918), 159-259.
14. BARKER, C. A. *Background of Revolution in Maryland.* New Haven, 1940.
15. BASSETT, John S. "The Regulators of North Carolina." *Am Hist Assn, Ann Rep,* 1894, 141-212.
16. BROWN, Robert E. *Middle-Class Democracy and the Revolution in Massachusetts, 1691-1780.* Ithaca, 1955.
17. BROWN, Robert E. and B. Katherine. *Virginia, 1705-1786: Democracy or Aristocracy.* Northport, Va., 1963.
18. BUEL, Richard, Jr. "Democracy and the American Revolution: A Frame of Reference." *Wm Mar Q,* 3d ser, XXI (1964), 165-190.
19. CARY, John and Robert E. BROWN. "Statistical Method and the Brown Thesis on Colonial Democracy." *Wm Mar Q,* 3d ser, XX (1963), 241-276.
20. CHAMPAGNE, Roger J. "Liberty Boys and Mechanics of New York City, 1764-1774." *Labor Hist,* VIII (1967), 115-135.
21. CHAMPAGNE, Roger J. "New York and the Intolerable Acts, 1774." *N Y Hist Soc Q,* XLV (1961), 195-207.

1. CHAMPAGNE, Roger J. "New York's Radicals and the Coming of Independence." *J Am Hist,* LI (1964), 21-40.
2. COLEMAN, Kenneth. *The American Revolution in Georgia, 1763-1789.* Athens, Ga., 1958.
3. DAVIDSON, Philip. "Sons of Liberty and Stamp Men." *N C Hist Rev,* IX (1932), 38-56.
4. DICKERSON, O. M. *The Navigation Acts and the American Revolution.* Philadelphia, 1951.†
5. DOUGLASS, Elisha P. *Rebels and Democrats: The Struggle for Equal Political Rights and Majority Rule during the American Revolution.* Chapel Hill, 1955.†
6. ENGELMAN, F. L. "Cadwallader Colden and the New York Stamp Act Riots." *Wm Mar Q,* 3d ser, X (1953), 560-578.
7. GIPSON, Lawrence H. "Aspects of the Beginning of the American Revolution in Massachusetts Bay, 1760-1762." *Proc Am Ant Soc,* LXVII (1957), 11-32.
8. GIPSON, Lawrence H. *The Coming of the Revolution, 1763-1775.* New York, 1954.†
9. HACKER, Louis M. "The First American Revolution." *Colum Univ Q,* XXXVII (1935), 259-295.
10. HARPER, Lawrence A. "Mercantilism and the American Revolution." *Can Hist Rev,* XXIII (1942), 1-15.
11. JENSEN, Merrill. "Democracy and the American Revolution." *Huntington Lib Q,* XX (1957), 321-341.
12. KLEIN, Milton M. "Review of Bernhard Knollenberg: Origin of the American Revolution, 1759-1766." *Wm Mar Q,* 3d ser, XVIII (1961), 277-280.
13. KNOLLENBERG, Bernhard. *Origin of the American Revolution, 1759-1766.* New York, 1960.†
14. LINCOLN, Charles H. *The Revolutionary Movement in Pennsylvania, 1760-1776. Ser Hist* (Penn), Philadelphia, 1901.
15. LOVEJOY, David S. *Rhode Island Politics and the American Revolution, 1760-1776.* Providence, 1958.
16. LYND, Staughton. "The Mechanics in New York City Politics, 1774-1788." *Labor Hist,* V (1964), 215-246.
17. MILLER, John C. *Origins of the American Revolution.* Boston, 1943.†
18. MORGAN, Edmund S. *The American Revolution: A Review of Changing Interpretations.* Washington, D.C., 1958.
19. MORGAN, Edmund S. and Helen. *The Stamp Act Crisis: Prologue to Revolution.* Chapel Hill, 1953.†
20. SACHS, W. S. "Interurban Correspondents and the Development of a National Economy before the Revolution: New York as a Case Study." *N Y Hist,* XXXVI (1955), 320-335.
21. SOSIN, Jack M. *Agents and Merchants: British Colonial Policy and the Origins of the American Revolution, 1763-1775.* Lincoln, Neb., 1965.
22. SOSIN, Jack M. *The Revolutionary Frontier, 1763-1783.* New York, 1967.†
23. SYDNOR, Charles S. *Gentlemen Freeholders.* Chapel Hill, 1952.†

THE COLONIAL PERIOD

1 TAYLOR, Robert J. *Western Massachusetts in the Revolution.* Providence, 1954.
2 THAYER, Theodore G. *Pennsylvania Politics and the Growth of Democracy, 1740-1776.* Harrisburg, 1953.
3 WALSH, Richard. *Charleston's Sons of Liberty: A Study of the Artisans, 1763-1789.* Columbia, S.C., 1959.
4 WARNER, Charles W. *Road to Revolution: Virginia's Rebels from Bacon to Jefferson (1676-1776).* Richmond, 1961.
5 WARREN, Winslow. "The Colonial Revenue Service in Massachusetts in its Relation to the Revolution." *Proc Mass Hist Soc,* XLVI (1912-1913), 440-474.
6 WASHBURN, Wilcomb E. *The Governor and the Rebel: A History of Bacon's Rebellion in Virginia.* Chapel Hill, 1957.†
7 WERTENBAKER, T. J. *Torchbearer of the American Revolution: The Story of Bacon's Rebellion and Its Leader.* Princeton, 1940.

V. The Early National Period, 1775–1820
1. General Studies

8 ADAMS, Henry C., ed. *The Writings of Albert Gallatin.* 3 vols. Philadelphia, 1879.
9 *American Railroad Journal. Steam Navigation, Commerce, Mining, Manufactures.* New York, 1832-1886.
10 BLODGET, Samuel. *Economica: A Statistical Manual for the United States of America.* Washington, D.C., 1806.
11 COLE, Arthur H., ed. *Industrial and Commercial Correspondence of Alexander Hamilton.* Chicago, 1928.
12 COXE, Tench. *View of the United States.* Philadelphia, 1794. Repr New York, 1965.
13 HAMILTON, Alexander. *Official Reports on Publick Credit, a National Bank, Manufactures, and a Mint.* Philadelphia, 1821.
14 LAMBERT, John. *Travels through Canada and the United States of North America in the Years 1806, 1807, and 1808.* 2 vols. 3d ed. London, 1816.
15 LA ROCHEFOUCAULD-LIANCOURT, F. A. *Travels through the United States of North America.* London, 1799.
16 *Niles' Weekly Register.* 76 vols. Baltimore, 1811-1849. (Titles varies.)
17 SEYBERT, Adam. *Statistical Annals of the United States, 1789-1818.* Philadelphia, 1818. Repr New York, 1967.
18 SYRETT, Harold C., and Jacob E. COOKE, eds. *The Papers of Alexander Hamilton.* 13 vols. New York, 1961-

EARLY NATIONAL PERIOD

1 TUCKER, George. *Progress of the United States in Population and Wealth in Fifty Years.* New York, 1843. (A convenient summary of decennial census data, 1790-1840.)

2 WINTERBOTHAM, William. *An Historical, Geographical, Commercial and Philosophical View of the American United States and of the European Settlements in America and the West Indies.* 4 vols. New York, 1795.

* * * * * * *

3 BJORK, Gordon C. "The Weaning of the American Economy: Independence, Market Changes, and Economic Development." *J Econ Hist,* XXIV (1964), 541-560. With comment by Albert Fishlow, 561-566.

4 Conference on Research in Income and Wealth. *Output, Employment, and Productivity in the United States after 1800.* Studies in Income and Wealth, XXX. New York, 1966.

5 Conference on Research in Income and Wealth. *Trends in the American Economy in the Nineteenth Century.* Studies in Income and Wealth, XXIV. Princeton, 1960.

6 DANGERFIELD, George. *The Era of Good Feelings.* New York, 1952.†

7 DAVID, Paul A. "The Growth of Real Product in the United States before 1840: New Evidence, Controlled Conjectures." *J Econ Hist,* XXVII (1967), 151-197.

8 DEPEW, C. M., ed. *One Hundred Years of American Commerce, 1795-1895.* 2 vols. New York, 1895.

9 DORFMAN, Joseph and R. G. TUGWELL. *Early American Policy: Six Columbia Contributors.* New York, 1960.

10 *Eighty Years Progress of the United States.* New York, 1867.

11 GOLDSMITH, Raymond W. "The Growth of Reproducible Wealth of the United States of America, 1805-1950," in *Income and Wealth in the United States, Trends and Structure.* Ed. by Simon Kuznets. Cambridge, Eng., 1952, 245-328. (International Association for Research in Income and Wealth. Income and Wealth Series II.)

12 GRIFFIN, Clifford S. *Their Brothers' Keepers: Moral Stewardship in the United States, 1800-1865.* New Brunswick, 1960.

13 HACKER, Louis M. *Alexander Hamilton in the American Tradition.* New York, 1957.

14 HUTCHESON, Harold. *Tench Coxe: A Study in American Economic Development.* Stud Hist Pol Sci (Hop). Baltimore, 1938.

15 KENYON, Cecilia M. "Alexander Hamilton: Rousseau of the Right." *Pol Sci Q,* LXXIII (1958), 161-178.

16 KUZNETS, Simon. "National Income Estimates for the United States prior to 1870." *J Econ Hist,* XII (1952), 115-130.

17 LAMB, Robert K. "The Entrepreneur and the Community." See 8.23, 91-119.

18 MARTIN, Robert F. *National Income in the United States, 1799-1938.* New York, 1939.

19 MILLER, John C. *Alexander Hamilton and the Growth of the New Nation.* New York, 1964.†

1 MITCHELL, Broadus. *Alexander Hamilton.* 2 vols. New York, 1957-1962.
2 MUDGE, E. T. *The Social Philosophy of John Taylor of Caroline.* New York, 1939.
3 NETTELS, Curtis P. *The Emergence of a National Economy, 1775-1815.* New York, 1962.† (Provides an extensive annotated bibliography.)
4 PARKER, William N. and Franklee WHARTENBY. "The Growth of Output before 1840," with comment by Samuel Rezneck. See **34**.5, 191-216.
5 PORTER, Kenneth W. *John Jacob Astor, Business Man. Stud Bus Hist* (Har). Ed. by N. S. B. Gras. 2 vols. Cambridge, Mass., 1931.
6 POULSON, Barry W. "Value Added in Manufacturing, Mining, and Agriculture in the American Economy from 1809 to 1839." Dissertation, Ohio State, 1965.
7 ROWE, Kenneth W. *Mathew Carey: A Study in American Economic Development. Stud Hist Pol Sci* (Hop). Baltimore, 1955.
8 SCHACHNER, Nathan. *Alexander Hamilton.* New York, 1946.†
9 TAYLOR, George Rogers. *The Transportation Revolution, 1815-1860.* New York, 1951.† (Provides an extensive, annotated bibliography.)
10 WALTERS, Raymond, Jr. *Albert Gallatin: Jeffersonian Financier and Diplomat.* New York, 1957.
11 WILTSE, Charles M. *The New Nation: 1800-1845.* New York, 1961.†

2. Regional and Local Studies

12 DE BOW, J. D. B. *Industrial Resources and Statistics of Southern and Western States.* 3 vols. New Orleans, 1852-1853.
13 DWIGHT, Timothy. *Travels in New England and New York.* 4 vols. New Haven, 1821-1822.
14 STODDARD, Major Amos. *Sketches, Historical and Descriptive, of Louisiana.* Philadelphia, 1812.

* * * * * * *

15 ADAMS, J. T. *New England in the Republic, 1776-1850.* Boston, 1926.
16 DAIN, Floyd R. *Every House a Frontier: Detroit's Economic Progress, 1815-1825.* Detroit, 1956.
17 FEE, Walter R. *The Transition from Aristocracy to Democracy in New Jersey, 1789-1829.* Somerville, N.J., 1933.
18 FOX, Dixon R. *The Decline of Aristocracy in the Politics of New York. Stud Hist Econ Pub Law* (Colum). New York, 1919.†
19 GEPHART, William F. *Transportation and Industrial Development in the Middle West. Stud Hist Econ Pub Law* (Colum). New York, 1909.
20 HARLOW, Ralph V. "Economic Conditions in Massachusetts during the American Revolution." *Pub Colo Soc Mass,* XX (1920), 163-190.
21 HUNTER, Louis C. "Studies in the Economic History of the Ohio Valley." *Stud Hist* (Smith), Northampton, Mass., 1933-1934, 6-130.
22 LUDLUM, D. M. *Social Ferment in Vermont, 1791-1850.* Montpelier, 1939.

1 MAIN, Jackson T. "The One Hundred." *Wm Mar Q*, 3d ser, XI (1954), 354-384. (The richest men of Virginia, 1780's.)

2 MAYER, Kurt B. *Economic Development and Population Growth in Rhode Island.* Providence, 1953.

3 MORISON, Samuel E. *Maritime History of Massachusetts, 1783-1860.* Boston, 1921.† (Authoratitive and delightfully written, a classic in the field of American economic history.)

4 MUNROE, John A. *Federalist Delaware, 1775-1815.* New Brunswick, 1954.

5 PELZER, Louis. "Economic Factors in the Aquisition of Louisiana." *Proc Miss Val Hist Assn*, VI (1912-1913), 109-127.

6 PURCELL, R. J. *Connecticut in Transition, 1775-1818.* Washington, D.C., 1918.

7 THOMPSON, R. T. *Colonel James Neilson: A Businessman of the Early Machine Age in New Jersey, 1784-1862.* New Brunswick, 1940.

3. Urban Studies

8 CRAIG, Neville B. *The History of Pittsburgh.* Pittsburgh, 1851.

9 DRAKE, Daniel. *Natural and Statistical View: Or Picture of Cincinnati and the Miami Country, Illustrated by Maps.* Cincinnati, 1815.

10 DWIGHT, Timothy. *A Statistical Account of the City of New Haven, 1811*

11 FORREST, William S. *Historical and Descriptive Sketches of Norfolk and Vicinity.* Philadelphia, 1853.

12 MEASE, James. *Picture of Philadelphia giving an Account of its Origin, Increase and Improvements in Arts, Sciences, Manufactures, Commerce and Revenue.* Philadelphia, 1811.

* * * * * * *

13 ALBION, Robert G. "New York Port and its Disappointed Rivals, 1815-1860." *J Econ Bus Hist*, III (1930-1931), 602-629.

14 BLAKE N. M. *Water for the Cities: A History of the Urban Water Supply Problem in the United States.* Syracuse, 1956.

15 GILCHRIST, David T., ed. *The Growth of the Seaport Cities, 1790-1825, Proceedings of a Conference Sponsored by the Eleutherian Mills—Hagley Foundation, March 17-19, 1966.* Charlottesville, Va., 1967.

16 GREEN, Constance McLaughlin. *History of Naugatuck, Connecticut.* New Haven, 1948.

17 GREEN, Constance McLaughlin. *Washington, Village and Capital, 1800-1878.* Princeton, 1963.

18 MC KELVEY, Blake. *Rochester: The Water-Power City, 1812-1854.* Cambridge, Mass., 1945. Repr Rochester, 1961.

19 MAYO, Bernard. "Lexington: Frontier Metropolis," in *Historiography and Urbanization. Essays in American History in Honor of W. Stull Holt.* Ed. by Eric F. Goldman. Baltimore, 1941, 21-42.

20 NEUFELD, Maurice. "Three Aspects of the Economic Life of Cincinnati from 1815 to 1840." *Ohio Arch Hist Q*, XLIV (1935), 65-80.

1 PRED, Allan R. *The Spatial Dynamics of U.S. Urban-Industrial Growth, 1800-1914: Interpretive and Theoretical Essays.* Cambridge, Mass., 1966.

2 REISER, Catherine E. *Pittsburgh's Commercial Development, 1800-1850.* Harrisburg, 1951.

3 RUBIN, Julius. "Urban Growth and Regional Development." See **36.15**, 3-21.

4 SPAULDING, E. Wilder. *New York in the Critical Period, 1783-1789.* New York, 1932.

5 STEVENS, Harry R. "Samuel Watts Davies and the Industrial Revolution in Cincinnati." *Ohio Hist Q,* LXX (1961), 95-127.

6 THERNSTROM, Stephan. *Poverty and Progress: Social Mobility in a Nineteenth Century City.* Ann Arbor, 1963. (City is Newburyport.)

7 WADE, Richard C. *The Urban Frontier: The Rise of Western Cities, 1790-1830.* Har Hist Mono. Cambridge, Mass., 1959.†

8 WADE, Richard C. "Urban Life in Western America, 1790-1830." *Am Hist Rev,* LXIV (1958), 14-30.

4. Population, Immigration, and Migration

9 BAHRET, James L. "Growth of New York and Suburbs since 1790." *Sci Monthly,* XI (1920), 404-418.

10 BERTHOFF, Rowland T. *British Immigrants in Industrial America, 1790-1950.* Cambridge, Mass., 1953.

11 DUBESTER, Henry J. *State Censuses: An Annotated Bibliography of Censuses of Population Taken after the Year 1790 by States and Territories of the United States.* Washington, D.C., 1948.

12 HANDLIN, Oscar. *Boston's Immigrants, 1790-1880: A Study in Acculturation.* Rev and enl ed. Cambridge, Mass., 1959.†

13 HEATON, Herbert. "The Industrial Immigrant in the United States, 1783-1812." *Proc Am Philos Soc,* XCV (1951), 519-527.

14 KLIMM, Lester E. *The Relation Between Certain Population Changes and the Physical Environment in Hampden, Hampshire and Franklin Counties, Massachusetts, 1790-1929.* Philadelphia, 1933.

15 LEE, Everett and Michael LALLI, with comments by George Rogers Taylor. "Population." See **36.15**, 25-46. (Analysis of urban population growth, 1770-1860.)

16 NIEHAUS, Earl F. *The Irish in New Orleans, 1800-1860.* Baton Rouge, 1965.

17 WILSON, Harold F. "Population Trends in Northwestern New England, 1790-1930." *Geog Rev,* XXIV (1934), 272-277.

5. Extractive Industry, Land Policy, and the Frontier

18 SCHOOLCRAFT, Henry R. *A View of the Lead Mines of Missouri.* New York 1819.

1 ARNDT, Karl J. R. *George Rapp's Harmony Society, 1785-1847.* Philadelphia, 1965.

2 BARNHART, John D. *Valley of Democracy: The Frontier Versus the Plantation in the Ohio Valley, 1775-1818.* Bloomington, Ind., 1953.

3 BIDWELL, Percy W. "The Agricultural Revolution in New England." *Am Hist Rev,* XXVI (1921), 683-702.

4 BIDWELL, Percy W. "Rural Economy in New England at the Beginning of the Nineteenth Century." *Tran Conn Acad Arts Sci,* XX (1916), 241-399.

5 BUCK, Solon J. "Frontier Economy in Southwestern Pennsylvania." *Ag Hist,* X (1936), 14-24.

6 BUCK, Solon J. *Illinois in 1818.* 2d rev ed. Chicago, 1918. (See chap v, "The Economic Situation.")

7 CATHEY, Cornelius O. *Agricultural Developments in North Carolina, 1783-1860.* Chapel Hill, 1956.

8 CHITTENDEN, Hiram M. *The American Fur Trade of the Far West.* 3 vols. Stanford, 1954.

9 COTTERILL, R. S. "The National Land System in the South: 1803-1812." *Miss Val Hist Rev,* XVI (1930), 495-506.

10 COTTERILL, R. S. "The South Carolina Land Cession." *Miss Val Hist Rev,* XII (1925), 376-384.

11 ELLIS, David M. *Landlords and Farmers in the Hudson-Mohawk Region, 1790-1850.* Ithaca, 1946.

12 ELLISWORTH, Lucius F. "The Philadelphia Society for the Promotion of Agriculture and Agricultural Reform, 1785-1793." *Ag Hist,* XLII (1968), 189-199.

13 GATES, Paul W. *The Farmer's Age: Agriculture, 1815-1860.* New York, 1960.† (Provides an extensive, annotated bibliography.)

14 HENDERSON, Elizabeth K. "The Northwestern Lands of Pennsylvania, 1790-1812." *Penn Mag Hist Biog,* LX (1936), 131-160.

15 HENLEIN, Paul C. *Cattle Kingdom in the Ohio Valley, 1783-1860.* Lexington, Ky., 1959.

16 HIBBARD, B. H. *A History of the Public Land Policies.* New York 1939.†

17 HOPKINS, James F. *History of the Hemp Industry in Kentucky.* Lexington, Ky., 1951.

18 INGALLS, W. R. *Lead and Zinc in the United States.* New York, 1908.

19 JENSEN, Merrill. "The Creation of the National Domain, 1781-1784." *Miss Val Hist Rev,* XXVI (1939), 323-342.

20 LAING, J. "The Early Development of the Coal Industry in the Western Counties of Virginia, 1800-1865." *W Va Hist,* XXVII (1966), 144-155.

21 LEAVITT, Charles T. "Transportation and the Livestock Industry of the Middle West to 1860." *Ag Hist,* VIII (1934), 20-33.

1 LE DUC, Thomas. "History and Appraisal of United States Land Policy to 1862," in *Land Use Policy and Problems in the United States.* Ed. by Howard W. Ottoson. Lincoln, Neb., 1963.

2 LEWIS, George E. *The Indiana Company, 1763-1798: A Study in Eighteenth Century Frontier Land Speculation and Business Venture.* Glendale, Calif., 1941.

3 LIVERMORE, Shaw. *Early American Land Companies: Their Influence on Corporate Development.* New York, 1939.

4 MC LENDON, James H. "The Development of Mississippi Agriculture: A Survey." *J Miss Hist,* XIII (1951), 75-87.

5 MC NALL, Neil A. *An Agricultural History of the Genesse Valley, 1790-1860.* Philadelphia, 1952.

6 MAIN, Jackson T. "The Distribution of Property in Post-Revolutionary Virginia." *Miss Val Hist Rev,* XLI (1954), 241-258.

7 MARTI, Donald B. "Early Agricultural Societies in New York: The Foundations of Improvement." *N Y Hist,* XLVIII (1967), 313-331.

8 MENDENHALL, Marjorie S. "A History of Agriculture in South Carolina, 1790 to 1860: An Economic and Social Study." Dissertation, Univ of N.C., 1940.

9 NUTE, Grace L. "The Papers of the American Fur Company: A Brief Estimate of Their Significance." *Am Hist Rev,* XXXII (1927), 519-538.

10 OGDEN, Adele. *The California Sea Otter Trade, 1784-1848.* Berkeley, 1941.

11 PARKMAN, Francis. *The Oregon Trail.* 8th rev ed. Boston, 1886.† (There have been many subsequent printings.)

12 PRATT, J. W. "Fur Trade Strategy and the American Left Flank in the War of 1812." *Am Hist Rev,* XL (1935), 246-273.

13 ROBBINS, Roy M. *Our Landed Heritage: The Public Domain, 1776-1936.* Princeton, 1942.†

14 ROBERT, Joseph C. *The Tobacco Kingdom: Plantation, Market and Factory in Virginia and North Carolina, 1800-1860.* Durham, N.C., 1938.

15 SCHAFER, Joseph. *The Wisconsin Lead Region.* Madison, 1932.

16 STEVENS, S. K. "When Timber was King in Pennsylvania." *Penn Hist,* XIX (1952), 391-396.

17 SWARTZLOW, Ruby J. "The Early History of Lead Mining in Missouri." *Mo Hist Rev,* XXVIII (1934), 184-194, 287-295, XXIX (1935), 27-34, 109-114, 195-205.

18 TOWNE, Marvin W. and Wayne D. RASMUSSEN. "Farm Gross Product and Gross Investment in the Nineteenth Century," with comment by Clarence H. Danhof. See 34.5, 255-315.

1 TREAT, Payson J. *National Land System, 1785-1820.* New York, 1910.
2 WAY, R. B. "The United States Factory System for Trading with the Indians, 1796-1822." *Miss Val Hist Rev,* VI (1919), 200-235.
3 WEINBERG, Albert K. *Manifest Destiny: A Study of Nationalist Expansionism in American History.* Baltimore, 1935.†
4 WHARTENBY, Franklee. "Land and Labor Productivity in the United States Cotton Production, 1800-1840." Dissertation, Univ of N.C., 1963.
5 WHITAKER, Arthur P. *The Spanish American Frontier, 1783-1795.* Boston, 1927

6. Transportation

6 COLLES, Christopher. *A Survey of the Roads of the United States of America 1789.* Ed. by Walter W. Ristow. Cambridge, Mass., 1961. (A facsimile reproduction of the earliest American road guide.)
7 POOR, Henry. *History of Railroads and Canals of the United States of America.* New York, 1860.

* * * * * * *

8 ALLEN, Turner W. "The Turnpike System in Kentucky: A Review of State Road Policy in the Nineteenth Century." *Filson Club Hist Q,* XXXVIII (1954), 239-259.
9 BALDWIN, Leland D. *The Keelboat Age on Western Water.* Pittsburgh, 1941.
10 CUMMINGS, Hubertis M. "Theodore Burr and His Bridges Across the Susquehanna." *Penn Hist,* XXIII (1956), 476-486.
11 CUTLER, Carl C. *Queens of the Western Ocean: The Story of America's Mail and Passenger Sailing Lines.* Annapolis, 1961.
12 DURRENBERGER, J. A. *Turnpikes: A Study of the Toll Road Movement in the Middle Atlantic States and Maryland.* Valdosta, Ga., 1931.
13 FLEXNER, James T. *Steamboat Come True: American Inventors in Action.* New York, 1944.
14 GRAY, Ralph D. *The National Waterway: A History of the Chesapeake and Delaware Canal, 1769-1965.* Urbana, 1967.
15 HARLOW, Alvin F. *Old Towpaths.* New York, 1926.
16 HARTSOUGH, M. L. *From Canoe to Steel Barge on the Upper Mississippi.* Minneapolis, 1934.
17 HATCHER, Harlan. *The Great Lakes.* New York, 1944.
18 HATCHER, Harlan. *Lake Erie.* New York, 1945.
19 HILL, Forest G. *Roads, Rails and Waterways: The Army Engineers and Early Transportation.* Norman, Okla., 1957.
20 HOAGLAND, H. E. "Early Transportation on the Mississippi before the Steamboat." *J Pol Econ,* XIX (1911), 111-123.
21 HOLMES, Oliver W. "The Turnpike Era," in *History of the State of New York.* New York, 1934, V, 257-294.

1 HOLMES, William F. "The New Castle and Frenchtown Turnpike and Railroad Company, 1809-1830: Part I, Turnpikes Across the Peninsula." *Del Hist,* X (1962), 71-104.

2 HUNTER, Robert F. "Turnpike Construction in Ante-Bellum Virginia." *Tech Cult,* IV (1963), 177-200.

3 JACKSON, Harry F. "The Utica Turnpike Road Company, 1804-1848." *N Y Hist,* XL (1959), 18-32.

4 JORDAN, Philip D. *The National Road.* Indianapolis, 1948. Repr Magnolia, Mass., 1967.

5 LANE, Wheaton J. *Commodore Vanderbilt: An Epic of the Steam Age.* New York, 1942.

6 LANE, Wheaton J. "The Turnpike Movement in New Jersey." *Proc N J Hist Soc,* LIII (1936), 19-52.

7 MARLOWE, George F. *Coaching Roads of Old New England.* New York, 1945.

8 MILLER, Nathan. *The Enterprise of a Free People: Aspects of Economic Development in New York State during the Canal Period, 1792-1838.* Ithaca, 1962.

9 MYERS, Richmond E. "The Early Turnpikes of the Susquehanna Valley." *Penn Hist,* XXI (1954), 248-259.

10 RAPP, Marvin A. "New York's Trade on the Great Lakes, 1800-1840." *N Y Hist,* XXXIX (1958), 22-33.

11 ROBERTS, Christopher. *The Middlesex Canal, 1793-1860. Har Econ Stud.* Cambridge, Mass., 1938.

12 SEARIGHT, T. B. *The Old Pike: A History of the National Road.* Uniontown, Pa., 1894.

13 TAYLOR, Philip E. "The Turnpike Era in New England." Dissertation, Yale Univ, 1934.

14 WINTHER, Oscar O. *The Transportation Frontier: Trans-Mississippi West, 1865-1890.* New York, 1964.

15 WOOD, Frederic J. *The Turnpikes of New England.* Boston, 1919.

7. *Commerce*

16 COXE, Tench. *A Brief Examination of Lord Sheffield's Considerations on the Commerce of the United States.* Philadelphia, 1791.

17 GALLATIN, Albert. "Report on Roads and Canals, Communicated to the Senate, Apr. 6, 1808." *American State Papers,* vol 37, *Miscellaneous* I, 724-921.

18 PITKIN, Timothy. *A Statistical View of the Commerce of the United States of America.* Hartford, 1816. 2d ed. New York, 1835.

19 SHEFFIELD, Lord John B. *Observations on the Commerce of the American States.* 6th ed. London, 1784.

* * * * * * *

1 ALBION, Robert G. "Maritime Adventures of New York in the Napoleonic Era," in *Essays in Modern English History in Honor of Wilbur Cortez Abbott.* Cambridge, Mass., 1941, 315-344.

2 ARENA, C. Richard, "Philadelphia-Mississippi Valley Trade and the Deposit Closure of 1802." *Penn Hist,* XXX (1963), 28-45.

3 ATHERTON, L. E. "Itinerant Merchandising in the Ante-Bellum South." *Bull Bus Hist Soc,* XIX (1945), 35-59.

4 BAMFORD, Paul W. "France and the American Market in Naval Timber and Masts, 1776-1786." *J Econ Hist,* XII (1952), 12-34.

5 BEMIS, S. F. *Jay's Treaty: A Study in Commerce and Diplomacy.* New York, 1923.†

6 BEMIS, S. F. *Pinckney's Treaty: A Study of American Advantage from Europe's Distress.* Baltimore, 1926.†

7 BENNETT, Norman R. and George E. BROOKS Jr., eds. *New England Merchants in Africa: A History Through Documents, 1802-1865.* Boston, 1965.

8 BENNS, Frank Lee. *The American Struggle for the West India Carrying Trade, 1815-1830.* Stud (Ind). Bloomington, Ind., 1923.

9 BJORK, Gordon C., with comments by Rhoda Dorsey and Robert A. Davison. "Foreign Trade." See **36**.15, 54-78. (Relates to Boston, New York, Philadelphia, and Baltimore.)

10 BRADLEE, Francis B. C. "Marblehead's Foreign Commerce, 1789-1850." *Essex Inst Hist Coll,* LXVI (1930), 97-123.

11 BRUCHEY, Stuart. *Robert Oliver, Merchant of Baltimore, 1783-1819.* Stud Hist Pol Sci (Hop). Baltimore, 1956.

12 BUCK, Norman S. *The Development of the Organization of Anglo-American Trade, 1800-1850.* New Haven, 1925.

13 BURON, Edmond. "Statistics on Franco-American Trade, 1778-1806." *J Econ Bus Hist,* IV (1932), 571-580.

14 BURT, A. L. *The United States, Great Britain and British North America.* New Haven, 1940.

15 CHANDLER, Charles L. "U.S. Merchant Ships in the Rio de la Plata (1801-1808) as Shown by Early Newspapers." *His-Am Hist Rev,* II (1919), 26, 50-51.

16 CHANDLER, Charles L. "U.S. Shipping in the La Plata Region, 1809-1811." *His-Am Hist Rev,* III (1920), 169-170.

17 CLAUDER, Anna C. *American Commerce as Affected by the Wars of the French Revolution and Napoleon, 1793-1812.* Philadelphia, 1932.

18 COATSWORTH, John H. "American Trade with European Colonies in the Caribbean and South America, 1790-1812." *Wm Mar Q,* 3d ser, XXIV (1967), 243-266.

19 CROSBY, Alfred W., Jr. *America, Russia, Hemp, and Napoleon: American Trade with Russia and the Baltic, 1783-1812.* Columbus, 1965.

20 DANIELS, G. W. "American Cotton Trade with Liverpool under the Embargo and Non-Intercourse Acts." *Am Hist Rev,* XXI (1916), 276-287.

21 DENNETT, Tyler. *Americans in Eastern Asia.* New York, 1941.

1 DIXON, F. H. *A Traffic History of the Mississippi River System.* Washington, D. C., 1909.

2 DORSEY, Rhoda M. "The Pattern of Baltimore Commerce during the Confederation Period." *Md Hist Mag,* LXII (1967), 119-134.

3 GALPIN, William F. "The American Grain Trade to the Spanish Peninsula, 1810-1814." *Am Hist Rev,* XXVIII (1922), 24-44.

4 GALPIN, William F. "The Grain Trade of New Orleans, 1804-1814." *Miss Val Hist Rev,* XIV (1928), 496-507.

5 GARES, Albert J. "Stephen Girard's West Indian Trade, 1789-1812." *Penn Mag Hist Biog,* LXXII (1948), 311-342.

6 IMLAH, Albert H. *Economic Elements in the Pax Britannica: Studies in British Foreign Trade in the Nineteenth Century.* Cambridge, Mass., 1958.

7 JENNINGS, Sister Marietta. *A Pioneer Merchant of St. Louis, 1810-1820.* Stud Hist Econ Pub Law (Colum), New York, 1939.

8 JONES, Fred M. "Middlemen in the Domestic Trade in the United States, 1800-1860." *Stud Soc Sci* (Ill). Urbana, 1937, 1-68.

9 KIMBALL, Gertrude S. *The East-India Trade of Providence from 1787-1807.* Providence, 1896.

10 KINDLEBERGER, C. P. "The United States Balance of Payments in the Nineteenth Century," a review of *American Growth and the Balance of Payments,* with reply by Jeffrey G. Williamson. *Explo Entrep Hist,* 2d ser, III (1965), 50-55.

11 KLINGAMAN, David. "The Development of Virginia's Coastwise Trade and Grain Trade in the Late Colonial Period." Dissertation, U of Va, 1967.

12 LIVINGOOD, James W. *The Philadelphia-Baltimore Trade Rivalry, 1780-1860.* Harrisburg, 1947.

13 LOSSE, Winifred J. "The Foreign Trade of Virginia, 1789-1809." *Wm Mar Q,* 3d ser, I (1944), 161-178.

14 LOVETT, Robert W. "A Tidewater Merchant in New Hampshire [George Frost, 1790-1830]." *Bus Hist Rev,* XXXIII (1959), 60-72.

15 MABRY, W. A. "Ante-Bellum Cincinnati and its Southern Trade." *American Studies in Honor of William Kenneth Boyd, by Members of the Americana Club of Duke University.* Durham, N.C., 1940, 60-85.

16 MC MASTER, John B. *The Life and Times of Stephen Girard.* 2 vols. Philadelphia, 1918.

17 MARBURG, Theodore, "Income Originating in Trade, 1799-1869." See **34.5**, 317-326.

18 NORRIS, Joe L. "The Country Merchant and the Industrial Magnate [Detroit, 1783-1930]." *Mich Hist,* XL (1956), 328-344.

19 NORTH, Douglass C. "The United States Balance of Payments, 1790-1860." See **34.5**, 573-627.

20 PETERSON, Merrill, "Thomas Jefferson and Commercial Policy, 1783-1793." *Wm Mar Q,* 3d ser, XXII (1965), 584-610.

1. PRATT, E. J. "Anglo-American Commercial and Political Rivalry on the Plata, 1820-1830." *His-Am Hist Rev,* II (1931), 302-335.
2. PUCKETT, Erastus P. "The Attempt of New Orleans to Meet the Crisis in Her Trade with the West." *Proc Miss Val Hist Assn,* X (1920-1921), 481-495.
3. RAGATZ, Lowell J. *The Fall of the Planter Class in the British Caribbean, 1763-1833.* New York, 1928.
4. RICH, Wesley E. *The History of the United States Post Office to the Year 1829. Har Econ Stud.* Cambridge, Mass., 1924.
5. RIPPY, J. F. *Rivalry of the United States and Great Britain over Latin America (1808-1830).* New York, 1964.
6. ROBERT, Joseph C. "Rise of the Tobacco Warehouse Auction System in Virginia, 1800-1860." *Ag Hist,* VII (1933), 170-182.
7. RUTTER, Frank R. *South American Trade of Baltimore. Stud Hist Pol Sci* (Hop). Baltimore, 1897.
8. SMITH, Philip C. F. "Crystal Blocks of Yankee Coldness: The Development of the Massachusetts Ice Trade from Frederick Tudor to Wenham Lake, 1806-1866." *Essex Inst Hist Coll,* XCVII (1960), 197-232.
9. STOVER, John F. "French-American Trade during the Confederation, 1781-1789." *N C Hist Rev,* XXXV (1958), 399-414.
10. THISTLETHWAITE, Frank. *The Anglo-American Connection in the Early Nineteenth Century.* Philadelphia, 1959.
11. TOOKER, Elva. *Nathan Trotter: Philadelphia Merchant, 1787-1853. Stud Bus Hist* (Har). Cambridge, Mass., 1955.
12. United States Treasury Department, Bureau of Statistics. *Statistical Tables Exhibiting the Commerce of the United States with European Countries from 1790 to 1890.* Washington, D. C., 1893.
13. WESTERFIELD, Ray B. "Early History of American Auctions—A Chapter in Commercial History." *Tran Conn Acad Arts Sci,* XXIII (1920), 159-210.
14. WHITAKER, Arthur P. *The Mississippi Question, 1795-1803: A Study in Trade, Politics, and Diplomacy.* New York, 1934.
15. WILDES, Harry E. *Lonely Midas: The Study of Stephen Girard.* New York, 1943.
16. WOODFOLK, George R. "Rival Urban Communication Schemes for the Possession of the Northwest Trade, 1783-1800." *Mid-America,* XXXVIII (1956), 214-232.
17. ZEIS, Paul M. *American Shipping Policy.* Princeton, 1938.

8. Manufacturing, Processing, and Building

18. APPLETON, Nathan. *The Introduction of the Power Loom and Origin of Lowell.* Lowell, Mass., 1858.
19. BATCHELDER, Samuel. *Introduction and Early Progress of the Cotton Manufacture in the United States.* Boston, 1863.

EARLY NATIONAL PERIOD

1 COXE, Tench. *A Statement of the Arts and Manufactures of the United States for 1810.* Philadelphia, 1814.

2 EVANS, Oliver. *The Young Millwright and Miller's Guide.* Philadelphia, 1795. (Fifteen editions 1795-1860 portray art and practice of water-milling.)

3 FRANCIS, W. H. *History of the Hatting Trade in Danbury Connecticut from its Commencement in 1780.* Danbury, 1860.

* * * * * * *

4 BALDWIN, Leland D. "Shipbuilding on the Western Waters, 1793-1817." *Miss Val Hist Rev,* XX (1933), 29-44.

5 BATHE, Greville and Dorothy. *Jacob Perkins: His Inventions, His Times, & His Contempories.* Philadelphia, 1943.

6 BATHE, Greville and Dorothy. *Oliver Evans: A Chronicle of Early American Engineering.* Philadelphia, 1935.

7 BATTISON, Edwin A. "Eli Whitney and the Milling Machine." *Smithsonian J Hist,* I (1966), 9-34.

8 BINING, Arthur C. "The Rise of Iron Manufacturing in Western Pennsylvania." *W Penn Hist Mag,* XVI (1933), 235-256.

9 BOYD, Thomas A. *Poor John Fitch: Inventor of the Steamboat.* New York, 1935.

10 BREWER, Thomas B. "The Formative Period of 140 American Manufacturing Companies, 1789-1929." Dissertation, U of Penn., 1962.

11 CALHOUN, Daniel H. *The American Civil Engineer: Origins and Conflict.* Cambridge, Mass., 1960. (An extensive bibliography.)

12 CLEMEN, R. A. *The American Livestock and Meat Industry.* New York, 1923.

13 COFFIN, Margaret. "The Fabulous Butlers of Brandy Hill." *N Y Hist,* XXXIV (1953), 351-360. (Tinsmiths, 1799-1860.)

14 COPELAND, Melvin T. *The Cotton Manufacture Industry of the United States.* Cambridge, Mass., 1912.

15 DE CAMP, L. Sprague. *The Heroic Age of American Invention.* Garden City, N.Y., 1961.

16 DEYRUP, Felicia J. "Arms Makers of the Connecticut Valley." *Stud Hist* (Smith). Northampton, Mass., 1948.

17 FULLER, Grace P. "An Introduction to the History of Connecticut as a Manufacturing State." *Stud Hist* (Smith). Northampton, Mass., 1915.

18 GIBB, George S. *The Saco-Lowell Shops: Textile Machinery Building in New England, 1813-1949. Stud Bus Hist* (Har). Cambridge, Mass., 1950.

19 GOODMAN, Paul. "Ethics and Enterprise: The Values of a Boston Elite, 1800-1860." *Am Q,* XVIII (1966), 437-451.

20 GRAY, Ralph D. "Transportation and Brandywine Industries, 1800-1840." *Del Hist,* IX (1961), 303-325.

21 GREEN, Constance McLaughlin. *Eli Whitney and the Birth of American Technology. The Library of American Biography.* Ed. by Oscar Handlin. Boston, 1956.†

1 GREGG, Dorothy. "John Stevens, General Entrepreneur." See 8.23, 120-152.
2 GRIFFIN, Richard W. "An Origin of the Industrial Revolution in Maryland: The Textile Industry, 1789-1826." *Md Hist Mag,* LXI (1966), 24-36.
3 HABAKKUK, H. J. *American and British Technology in the Nineteenth Century: The Search for Labour-Saving Inventions.* New York, 1962.†
4 HALL, Courtney R. *History of American Industrial Science.* New York, 1954.
5 HAMMOND, Seth. "The Ante-Bellum Kentucky Cotton Industry, 1790-1860." *Cotton Hist Rev,* I (1960), 47-55.
6 HANCOCK, Harold B. and Norman B. WILKINSON. "The Gilpins and Their Endless Paper Machine." *Penn Mag Hist Biog,* LXXXI (1957), 391-405.
7 HANNAY, Agnes. *A Chronicle of Industry on the Mill River.* Stud Hist (Smith). Northampton, Mass., 1936.
8 HERNDON, G. M. "A War-Inspired Industry: The Manufacture of Hemp in Virginia during the Revolution." *Va Mag Hist Biog,* LXXIV (1966), 301-311.
9 HUTCHINS, John G. B. *The American Maritime Industries and Public Policy, 1789-1914.* Har Econ Stud. Cambridge, Mass., 1941.
10 ISARD, Walter. "Some Locational Factors in the Iron and Steel Industry Since the Early Nineteenth Century." *J Pol Econ,* LVI (1948), 203-217.
11 LANDER, Ernest M., Jr. "Ante-Bellum Milling in South Carolina." *S C Hist Genea Mag,* LII (1951), 125-132.
12 LANDER, Ernest M., Jr. "The Iron Industry in Ante-Bellum South Carolina." *J S Hist,* XX (1954), 337-355.
13 LANDES, David. "Factor Costs and Demand: Determinants of Economic Growth: A Critique of Professor Habakkuk's Thesis." *Bus Hist Rev,* VII (1965), 15-33.
14 LATHROP, W. G. *The Brass Industry in Connecticut.* Shelton, Conn., 1909.
15 LEYLAND, H. T. "Early Years of the Hope Cotton Manufacturing Company." *R I Hist,* XXV (1966), 25-32.
16 LINCOLN, Jonathan T. "The Beginnings of the Machine Age in New England: David Wilkinson of Pawtucket." *N Eng Q,* VI (1933), 716-732. (Early manufacture of machinery and machine tools.)
17 LOVETT, Robert W. "The Beverly Cotton Manufactory: Or Some New Light on an Early Cotton Mill (1789-1798)." *Bull Bus Hist Soc,* XXVI (1952), 218-237.
18 MC CORISON, Marcus A. "Vermont Papermaking, 1784-1820." *Vt Hist,* XXXI (1963), 209-245.
19 MC GOULDRICK, Paul F. *New England Textiles in the Nineteenth Century.* Har Econ Stud. Cambridge, Mass., 1968.
20 MAILLOUX, Kenneth. "The Boston Manufacturing Company." *Textile Hist Rev,* IV (1963), 157-163; V (1964), 3-29.
21 MIRSKEY, J. and Allan NEVINS. *The World of Eli Whitney.* New York, 1952.†

1 MORISON, Samuel E. *The Ropemakers of Plymouth: A History of the Plymouth Cordage Co., 1824-1949.* Boston, 1950.

2 MURPHY, John J. "Entrepreneurship in the Establishment of the American Clock Industry." *J Econ Hist,* XXVI (1966), 169-186.

3 STANDARD, Diffee and Richard W. GRIFFIN. "The Cotton Textile Industry in Ante-Bellum North Carolina." Part I, "Origin and Growth to 1830." *N C Hist Rev,* XXXIV (1957), 15-35.

4 STRASSMANN, W. Paul, *Risk and Technological Innovations: American Manufacturing Methods During the Nineteenth Century.* Ithaca, 1959.

5 TABER, Martha V. *A History of the Cutlery Industry in the Connecticut Valley. Stud Hist* (Smith). Northampton, Mass., 1955.

6 TURNBULL, Archibold D. *John Stevens, An American Record.* New York, 1928.

7 WARE, Caroline F. *The Early New England Cotton Manufacture: A Study in Industrial Beginnings.* Boston, 1931.

8 WILKINSON, Norman B. "Brandywine Borrowings from European Technology." *Tech Cult,* IV (1963), 1-13.

9 WOODBURY, Robert S. "The Legend of Eli Whitney and Interchangeable Parts." *Tech Cult,* I (1960), 235-253.

9. Labor

10 COMMONS, John R. and Eugene A. GILMORE. *Labor Conspiracy Cases, 1806-1842.* See **7**.1, vols 3-4.

* * * * * * *

11 ADAMS, Donald R., Jr. "Wage Rates in the Early National Period: Philadelphia, 1785-1830." *J Econ Hist,* XXVIII (1968), 404-417.

12 DU BOIS, W. E. B. and Augustus G. DILL. *The Negro American Artisan.* Atlanta, 1912.

13 FRANKLIN, John H. *The Free Negro in North Carolina, 1790-1860.* Chapel Hill, 1943.

14 GIBSON, George H. "Labor Piracy on the Brandywine." *Labor Hist,* VIII (1967), 175-182. (Three interesting examples, 1808-1809, 1811-1812, and 1822.)

15 LANDER, Ernest M., Jr. "Slave Labor in South Carolina Cotton Mills." *J Neg Hist,* XXXVIII (1953), 161-173.

16 LEBERGOTT, Stanley. "Labor Force and Employment, 1800-1960," with comment by Brinley Thomas. See **34**.4, 117-210.

17 LEBERGOTT, Stanley. *Manpower in Economic Growth: The American Record Since 1800.* New York, 1964.

18 LEBERGOTT, Stanley. "Wage Trends, 1800-1900," with comment by Albert Rees. See **34**.5, 449-499.

19 MC COLLEY, Robert. *Slavery and Jeffersonian Virginia.* Urbana, 1964. (Demonstrates slavery was not dying in Virginia, 1775-1812, as some have claimed.)

20 MONTGOMERY, David. "The Working Classes of the Pre-Industrial American City, 1780-1830." *Labor Hist,* IX (1968), 3-22.

21 SCHMIDT, Martin F. "The Early Printers of Louisville, 1800-1860." *Filson Club Hist Q,* XL (1966), 307-334.

1 SULLIVAN, William A. *The Industrial Worker in Pennsylvania, 1800-1840.* Harrisburg, 1955.

2 TAFT, Philip. *Organized Labor in American History.* New York, 1964.

3 TAYLOR, Rosser H. *Slaveholding in North Carolina: An Economic View.* Chapel Hill, 1926.

4 TRACY, George A., comp. *History of the Typographical Union.* Indianapolis, 1913.

10. *Finance*

A. PUBLIC FINANCE

5 GALLATIN, Albert. *Writings of Albert Gallatin.* Ed. Henry C. Adams. 3 vols. Philadelphia, 1879.

* * * * * * *

6 ADAMS, Henry C. *Taxation in the United States, 1789-1816. Stud Hist Pol Sci* (Hop). Baltimore, 1884.

7 BALINKY, Alexander S. *Albert Gallatin, Fiscal Theories and Policies.* New Brunswick, 1958.

8 BARBER, William D. "'Among the most Techy Articles of Civil Police': Federal Taxation and the Adoption of the Whiskey Excise." *Wm Mar Q,* 3d ser, XXV (1968), 59-84.

9 BAYLEY, Rafael A. *The National Loans of the United States, from July 4, 1776 to June 30, 1880.* Washington, D. C., 1881.

10 BOGART, Ernest L. *Financial History of Ohio.* Urbana, 1912.

11 BOLLES, Albert S. *The Financial History of the United States from 1789 to 1860.* 2d ed. New York, 1885.

12 BRUCHEY, Stuart. "The Forces behind the Constitution: A Critical Review of the Framework of E. James Ferguson's *The Power of the Purse.*" *Wm Mar Q,* 3d ser, XIX (1962), 429-438.

13 BULLOCK, Charles J. *The Finances of the United States from 1775 to 1789. Econ Pol Sci Ser* (Wis). Madison, 1895.

14 COLLIER, Christopher. "Continental Bonds in Connecticut on the Eve of the Funding Measure." *Wm Mar Q,* 3d ser, XXII (1965), 646-651.

15 FERGUSON, E. James. *The Power of the Purse: A History of American Public Finance, 1776-1790.* Chapel Hill, 1961. (Contains a useful, annotated bibliography.)

16 JEWETT, Fred E. *A Financial History of Maine.* New York, 1937.

17 KIMMEL, Lewis H. *Federal Budget and Fiscal Policy, 1789-1958.* Washington, D. C., 1959.

18 OBERHOLTZER, Ellis P. *Robert Morris: Patriot and Financier.* New York, 1903.

19 SCHEIBER, Harry N. "The Condition of American Federalism: An Historian's View." Committee on Government Operations United States Senate. 89th Congress, 2d Sess. Washington, D.C., 1966. (Federal grants-in-aid.)

1 SOWERS, Don C. *The Financial History of New York State form 1789 to 1912. Stud Hist Econ Pub Law* (Colum). New York, 1914.

2 SUMNER, William G. *The Financier and Finances of the American Revolution.* New York, 1891. Repr New York, 1966.

3 SWANSON, Donald F. *The Origins of Hamilton's Fiscal Policies.* Gainesville, Fla., 1963.

4 TAUS, Esther R. *Central Banking Functions of the United States Treasury, 1789-1941.* New York, 1943.

5 TAYLOR, George Rogers, ed. *Hamilton and the National Debt.* Boston, 1950.† (Readings).

6 TRESCOTT, Paul B. "The United States Government and National Income, 1790-1860." See **34.5**, 337-361.

7 United States Bureau of the Census. *Tenth Census, 1880, VII, Valuation, Taxation, and Public Indebtedness.* Washington, D.C., 1884, 521-645. (For a detailed history of the public debt, see 521-645.)

8 VER STEEG, Clarence L. *Robert Morris: Revolutionary Financier, with an Analysis of his Earlier Career.* Philadelphia, 1954.

9 WOOD, Frederick A. *History of Taxation in Vermont.* New York, 1894.

B. MONEY AND FINANCIAL INSTITUTIONS

10 RAGUET, Condy. *An Inquiry into the Causes of the Present State of the Circulating Medium.* Philadelphia, 1815.

11 WEBSTER, Pelatiah. *Political Essays on the Nature and Operation of Money, Public Finances and Other Subjects.* Philadelphia, 1791.

12 WOLCOTT, Oliver. *Remarks on the Present State of the Currency.* New York, 1820.

* * * * * * *

13 AITKEN, Hugh G. J. "Yates and McIntyre: Lottery Managers [1821-1834]." *J Econ Hist,* XIII (1953), 36-57.

14 BROWN, John C. *One Hundred Years of Merchant Banking.* New York, 1909.

15 CALDWELL, Stephen A. *A Banking History of Louisiana.* Baton Rouge, 1935.

16 CAROTHERS, Neil. *Fractional Money.* New York, 1930.

17 CARTER, E. C., II. "The Birth of a Political Economist: Mathew Carey and the Recharter Fight of 1810-1811." *Penn Hist,* XXXIII (1966), 274-288.

18 CHADBOURNE, W. W. *A History of Banking in Maine, 1799-1930.* Orono, Me., 1936.

19 CHADDOCK, Robert E. *The Safety Fund Banking System in New York, 1829-1866.* Washington, D.C., 1910.

20 DAVIS, Lance E. and J. R. T. HUGHES. "A Dollar-Sterling Exchange, 1803-1895." *Econ Hist Rev,* 2d ser, XII (1960), 52-78.

EARLY NATIONAL PERIOD

1. DEWEY, Davis R. *State Banking before the Civil War.* Washington, D.C., 1910.
2. ESAREY, Logan. *State Banking in Indiana, 1814-1873.* Bloomington, Ind., 1912.
3. FENSTERMAKER, J. Van. *The Development of American Commercial Banking, 1782-1837.* Kent, Ohio, 1965.
4. FENSTERMAKER, J. Van. "The Statistics of American Commercial Banking, 1782-1818." *J Econ Hist,* XXV (1965), 400-413.
5. FOULDS, Margaret H. "The Massachusetts Bank, 1784-1865." *J Econ Bus Hist,* II (1930), 256-270.
6. GRAS, N. S. B. *The Massachusetts-First National Bank of Boston, 1784-1934.* Stud Bus Hist (Har). Cambridge, Mass., 1937.
7. HELDERMAN, Leonard C. *National and State Banks.* Boston, 1931.
8. HEPBURN, A. B. *A History of Currency in the United States.* New York, 1924. Repr New York, 1967.
9. HOLDSWORTH, John T. and Davis R. DEWEY. *The First and Second Banks of the United States.* Washington, D.C., 1911.
10. HUNTINGTON, C. C. *A History of Banking and Currency in Ohio before the Civil War. Ohio Arch Hist Q.* Columbus, 1915.
11. KROOSS, Herman E., with comments by Stuart Bruchey. "Financial Institutions." See **36.**15, 104-143. (Developments in Boston, New York, Philadelphia, and Baltimore.)
12. LAKE, Wilfred S. "The End of the Suffolk System." *J Econ Hist,* VII (1947), 183-207.
13. MARTIN, J. G. *Seventy-Three Years History of the Boston Stock Market (1798-1871).* Boston, 1871.
14. MORGAN, H. Wayne. "The Origins and Establishment of the First Bank of the United States." *Bus Hist Rev,* XXX (1956), 472-492.
15. NEVINS, Allan. *History of the Bank of New York and Trust Company, 1784 to 1934.* New York, 1934.
16. NUSSBAUM, Arthur. *A History of the Dollar.* New York, 1957.
17. REDLICH, Fritz. *The Molding of American Banking: Men and Ideas.* 2 vols. New York, 1951.
18. SPARKS, Earl S. *History and Theory of Agricultural Credit in the United States.* New York, 1932.
19. STEVENS, Harry R. "Bank Enterprisers in a Western Town 1815-1822." *Bus Hist Rev,* XXIX (1955), 139-156. (Cincinnati.)
20. TRESCOTT, Paul B. *Financing American Enterprise: The Story of Commercial Banking.* New York, 1963.
21. WAINWRIGHT, Nicholas B. *History of the Philadelphia National Bank, 1803-1953.* Philadelphia, 1953.
22. WETTEREAU, James O. "The Branches of the First Bank of the United States." *J Econ Hist,* II (1942), 66-100.
23. WETTEREAU, James O. "New Light on the First Bank of the United States." *Penn Mag Hist Biog,* LXI (1937), 263-285.

1 WHITE, Gerald T. *A History of the Massachusetts Hospital Life Insurance Company.* Cambridge, Mass., 1955.

C. PRICES AND BUSINESS CONDITIONS

2 ADAMS, T. M. *Prices Paid by Farmers for Goods and Services and Received by them for Farm Products, 1790-1871: Wages of Farm Labor, 1780-1937.* Burlington, Vt., 1939.

3 BERRY, Thomas. *Western Prices before 1861: A Study of the Cincinnati Market.* Har Econ Stud. Cambridge, Mass., 1943.

4 BEZANSON, Anne. *Prices and Inflation during the American Revolution, 1770-1790.* Philadelphia, 1951.

5 BEZANSON, Anne, Robert D. GRAY, and M. HUSSEY. *Wholesale Prices in Philadelphia, 1784-1861.* 2 vols. Philadelphia, 1936-1937.

6 BJORK, Gordon C. "Stagnation and Growth in the American Economy: 1784-1792." Dissertation, U of Wash., 1963.

7 BRADY, Dorothy S. "Price Deflators for Final Product Estimates." See 34.4, 91-115.

8 BRADY, Dorothy S. "Relative Prices in the Nineteenth Century." *J Econ Hist,* XXIV (1964), 145-203.

9 COMETTI, Elizabeth. "Inflation in Revolutionary Maryland." *Wm Mar Q,* 3d ser, VIII (1951), 228-234.

10 DORSEY, Dorothy B. "The Panic of 1819 in Missouri." *Mo Hist Rev,* XXIX (1935), 79-91.

11 GREER, Thomas H. "Economic and Social Effects of the Depression of 1819 in the Old Northwest." *Ind Mag Hist,* XLIV (1948), 227-243.

12 PETERSON, Arthur G. *Historical Study of Prices Received by Producers of Farm Products in Virginia, 1801-1927.* Washington, D.C., 1929.

13 REZNECK, Samuel. "Depression of 1819-1822: A Social History." *Am Hist Rev,* XXXIX (1933), 28-47.

14 ROTHBARD, Murray N. *The Panic of 1819.* Stud Hist Econ Pub Law (Colum). New York, 1962.

15 SMITH, Walter B. and Arthur H. COLE. *Fluctuations in American Business, 1790-1860.* Har Econ Stud. Cambridge, Mass., 1935.

16 SOBEL, Robert. *The Big Board: A History of the New York Stock Market.* New York, 1965.†

17 TAYLOR, George Rogers. "Prices in the Mississippi Valley Preceding the War of 1812." *J Econ Bus Hist,* III (1930), 148-163.

18 TAYLOR, George Rogers. "Wholesale Commodity Prices at Charleston, South Carolina, 1796-1861." *J Econ Bus Hist,* IV (1932), 848-876.

19 THORP, Willard. *Business Annals.* New York, 1926.

11. *Corporations and Government-Business Relations*

20 TAUSSIG, F. W. *State Papers and Speeches on the Tariff.* Cambridge, Mass., 1893.

* * * * * * *

52 EARLY NATIONAL PERIOD

1 BLANDI, Joseph G. *Maryland Business Corporations, 1783-1852. Stud Hist Pol Sci* (Hop). Baltimore, 1934.

2 CADMAN, John W., Jr. *The Corporation in New Jersey: Business and Politics, 1791-1875.* Cambridge, Mass., 1949.

3 CALLENDER, Guy Stevens. "The Early Transportation and Banking Enterprises of the States in Relation to the Growth of Corporations." *Q J Econ,* XVII (1902), 111-162.

4 DAVIS, Joseph S. *Essays in the Earlier History of American Corporations.* Cambridge, Mass., 1917.

5 DODD, Merrick E. "The Evolution of Limited Liability in Massachusetts." *Proc Mass Hist Soc,* LXVIII (1946), 228-256.

6 ELAZAR, Daniel J. *The American Partnership, Intergovernment Cooperation in the Nineteenth-Century United States.* Chicago, 1962. (Emphasizes that virtually all activities were shared by federal and state agencies.)

7 ELLIOTT, Orrin L. *The Tariff Controversy in the United States 1789-1833.* Palo Alto, Calif., 1892.

8 EVANS, G. H. Jr. *Business Incorporations in the United States, 1800-1943.* New York, 1948.

9 GOODRICH, Carter. *The Government and the Economy, 1783-1861.* New York, 1967.

10 GOODRICH, Carter. *Government Promotion of American Canals and Railways, 1800-1890.* New York, 1960.

11 HANDLIN, Oscar. *Commonwealth: A Study of the Role of Government in the American Economy, Massachusetts, 1774-1861.* New York, 1947,

12 HANDLIN, Oscar and Mary. "Origins of the American Business Corporation." *J Econ Hist,* V (1945), 1-23.

13 HARTZ, Louis. *Economic Policy and Democratic Though: Pennsylvania, 1776-1860.* Cambridge, Mass., 1948.

14 HEATH, Milton. *Constructive Liberalism: The Role of the State in Economic Development in Georgia to 1860.* Cambridge, Mass., 1954.

15 KAISER, Carl W., Jr. *History of the Academic Protectionist-Free Trade Controversy in America before 1860.* Philadelphia, 1939.

16 KESSLER, W. C. "Incorporation in New England: A Statistical Study, 1800-1875." *J Econ Hist,* VIII (1948), 43-62.

17 KESSLER, W. C. "A Statistical Study of the New York General Incorporation Act of 1811." *J Pol Econ,* XLVIII (1940), 877-882.

18 LIVERMORE, Shaw. "Unlimited Liability in Early American Corporations." *J Pol Econ,* XLIII (1935), 674-687.

19 MILLER, William. "A Note on the History of Business Corporations in Pennsylvania, 1800-1860." *Q J Econ,* LV (1940), 150-160.

20 PREYER, Norris W. "Southern Support of the Tariff of 1816: A Reappraisal." *J S Hist,* XXV (1959), 306-322.

21 SCHWARTZ, Anna J. "Gross Dividend and Interest Payments by Corporations at Selected Dates in the Nineteenth Century," with comment by John G. Gurley. See **34.5**, 407-448.

1 STANWOOD, Edward. *American Tariff Controversies in the Nineteenth Century.* New York, 1903.

2 TAUSSIG, F. W. *The Tariff History of the United States.* New York, 1888.† (The first of numerous editions.)

3 WARREN, Charles. *Bankruptcy in United States History.* Cambridge, Mass., 1935.

4 WESLEY, Edgar B. "The Government Factory System among the Indians 1795-1822." *J Econ Bus Hist,* IV (1932), 487-511.

5 WRIGHT, Chester W. *Wool-Growing and the Tariff. Har Econ Stud.* Boston, 1910.

6 ZORNOW, William F. "Massachusetts Tariff Policies, 1775-1789." *Essex Inst Hist Coll,* XC (1954), 194-216.

7 ZORNOW, William F. "The Tariff Policies of Virginia, 1775-1789." *Va Mag Hist Biog,* LXII (1954), 306-319.

12. Economic Aspects of Major Political Developments

A. THE REVOLUTION, 1776-1783

8 COWL, Philip A. *Maryland During and After the Revolution.* Baltimore, 1943.

9 EAST, Robert A. *Business Enterprise in the American Revolutionary Era. Stud Hist Econ Pub Law* (Colum). New York, 1938.

10 EAST, Robert A. "The Massachusetts Conservatives in the Critical Period." See 17.13, 349-390.

11 FERGUSON, E. James. "Business, Government, and Congressional Investigation in the Revolution." *Wm Mar Q,* 3d ser, XVI (1959), 293-318.

12 FINGERHUT, Eugene R. "Uses and Abuses of the American Loyalists' Claims: a Critique of Quantitative Analyses." *Wm Mar Q,* 3d ser, XXV (1968), 245-258.

13 JAMESON, John F. *The American Revolution Considered as a Social Movement.* Princeton, 1926.†

14 JOHNSON, Victor L. *The Administration of the American Commissariat During the Revolutionary War.* Philadelphia, 1941.

15 MC DONALD, Forrest.. *E. Pluribus Unum: The Formation of the American Republic, 1776-1790.* Boston, 1965.†

16 MAIN, Jackson T. "Government by the People, the American Revolution and the Democratization of the Legislatures." *Wm Mar Q,* 3d ser, XXIII (1966), 391-407.

17 MAIN, Jackson T. *The Social Structure of Revolutionary America.* Princeton, 1965.

18 MASON, B. "Entrepreneurial Activity in New York during the American Revolution." *Bus Hist Rev,* XL (1966), 190-212.

19 MORRIS, Richard B., ed. *The Era of the American Revolution.* See 17.13.†

1 NEVINS, Allan. *The American States during and after the Revolution, 1775-1789.* New York, 1924.

2 NEWCOMER, Lee N. *The Embattled Farmers: A Massachusetts Countryside in the American Revolution.* New York, 1953.

3 PINKETT, Harold T. "Maryland as a Source of Food Supplies during the American Revolution." *Md Hist Mag,* XLVI (1951), 157-172.

4 VER STEEG, Clarence L. "The American Revolution Considered as an Economic Movement." *Huntington Lib Q,* XX (1957), 361-372. (Treats the economic results of the Revolution.)

5 WOOD, Gordon S. "Rhetoric and Reality in the American Revolution." *Wm Mar Q,* 3d ser, XXIII (1966), 1-32.

B. THE CONFEDERATION AND THE ADOPTION OF THE CONSTITUTION, 1784-1789

6 BEARD, Charles A. *An Economic Interpretation of the Constitution of the United States.* New York, 1913.†

7 BROGAN, D. W. "The Quarrel over Charles Austin Beard and the American Constitution." *Econ Hist Rev,* 2d ser, XVIII (1965), 199-223.

8 BROWN, Robert E. *Charles Beard and the Constitution: A Critical Analysis of an Economic Interpretation of the Constitution.* Princeton, 1956.†

9 DYER, Walter A. "Embattled Farmers." *N Eng Q,* IV (1931), 460-481. (Shays' Rebellion.)

10 ELKINS, Stanley and Eric MC KITRICK. "The Founding Fathers, Young Men of the Revolution." *Pol Sci Q,* LXXVI (1961), 181-216. (An appraisal of interpretations of the factors involved in the adoption of the Constitution.)

11 FISKE, John. *The Critical Period, 1783-1789.* Boston, 1888.

12 GOODMAN, Paul. *The Democratic-Republicans of Massachusetts: Politics in a Young Republic.* Cambridge, Mass., 1964.

13 HUNTER, William C. *The Commercial Policy of New Jersey under the Confederation, 1783-1789.* Princeton, 1922.

14 JENSEN, Merrill. *The New Nation, A History of the United States during the Confederation, 1781-1789.* New York, 1950.†

15 LIBBY, O. G. *The Geographical Distribution of the Vote of the Thirteen States on the Federal Constitution, 1787-1788.* Madison, 1894.

16 MC DONALD, Forrest. *We the People: The Economic Origins of the Constitution.* Chicago, 1958.†

17 MAIN, Jackson T. *The Anti-Federalists: Critics of the Constitution, 1781-1788.* Chapel Hill, 1961.†

18 MAIN, Jackson T. "Sections and Politics in Virginia, 1781-1787." *Wm Mar Q,* 3d ser, XII (1955), 96-112.

19 MORRIS, Richard B. "Class Struggle and the American Revolution." *Wm Mar Q,* 3d ser, XIX (1962), 3-29.

20 MORRIS, Richard B. "The Confederation Period and the American Historian." *Wm Mar Q,* 3d ser, XIII (1956), 139-156.

1 SCHAFFER, Allan. "Virginia's 'Critical Period.'" See **19**.10, 152-170.
2 TAILBY, Donald G. "Foreign Interest Remittances by the United States, 1785-1787: A Story of Malfeasance." *Bus Hist Rev,* XLI (1967), 161-176.

C. THE NEW NATION, 1790-1820

3 MANNING, William. *The Key of Libberty.* Ed. Samuel E. Morison. Billerica, Mass., 1922. (Thoughts on post-Revolutionary War problems by a dirt farmer. Written 1798.)

* * * * * * *

4 BEARD, Charles A. *Economic Origins of Jeffersonian Democracy.* New York, 1927.†
5 BOWMAN, Albert H. "Jefferson, Hamilton and American Foreign Policy." *Pol Sci Q,* LXXI (1956), 18-41.
6 COOKE, Jacob E. "The Whiskey Insurrection: A Re-Evaluation." *Penn Hist,* XXX (1963), 316-346.
7 GOODMAN, Warren H. "The Origins of the War of 1812: A Survey of Changing Interpretations." *Miss Val Hist Rev,* XXVIII (1941), 171-186.
8 GRAMPP, William D. "A Re-examination of Jeffersonian Economics." *S Econ J,* XII (1946), 363-382.
9 HORSMAN, Reginald. *The Causes of the War of 1812.* Philadelphia, 1962.†
10 JENNINGS, Walter W. *The American Embargo, 1807-1809.* Iowa City, 1921.
11 LATIMER, Margaret K. "South Carolina—A Protagonist of the War of 1812." *Am Hist Rev,* LXI (1956), 914-929.
12 PERKINS, Bradford, ed. *The Causes of the War of 1812: National Honor or National Interest?* New York, 1962.† (Readings.)
13 PERKINS, Broadford. *Prologue to War: England and the United States, 1805-1812.* Berkeley, 1961.
14 PRATT, J. W. *Expansionists of 1812.* New York, 1925.
15 RISJORD, Norman K. "1812: Conservatives, War Hawks, and the Nation's Honor." *Wm Mar Q,* 3d ser, XVIII (1961), 196-210.
16 RUBIN, Israel I. "New York State and the Long Embargo." Dissertation, New York U, 1961.
17 SEARS, Louis M. *Jefferson and the Embargo, 1927.* Durham, N.C., 1927.
18 TAYLOR, George Rogers. "Agrarian Discontent in the Mississippi Valley Preceding the War of 1812." *J Pol Econ,* XXXIX (1931), 471-505.
19 TAYLOR, George Rogers, ed. *The War of 1812, Past Justifications and Present Interpretations.* Boston, 1963.† (Readings.)
20 WALFORD, Thorp L. "Democratic-Republican Reaction in Massachusetts to the Embargo of 1807." *N Eng Q,* XV (1942), 35-61.

VI. The Era of Accelerated Growth, 1820–1860

1. General Contemporary Materials

1 ANDREWS, Israel D. *The Trade and Commerce of the British North American Colonies.* Washington, D.C., 1854.

2 CHASE, Henry and C. H. SANBORN. *The North and the South: A Statistical View of the Condition of the Free and the Slave States.* New York, 1857.

3 CHEVALIER, Michael. *Society, Manners and Politics in the United States.* Boston, 1839.†

4 DE BOW, J. D. B. *Statistical View of the United States being a Compendium of the Seventh Census.* Washington, D.C., 1854.

5 *De Bow's Commercial Review of the South and West.* 1-39 vols. New Orleans, 1846-1870. (Title varies.)

6 HAYWARD, John. *Gazetteer of the United States.* Hartford, 1853.

7 *Hazard's Register of Pennsylvania.* 16 vols. Philadelphia, 1828-1835.

8 *Hazard's United States Commercial and Statistical Register.* 6 vols. Philadelphia, 1839-1842.

9 MC CULLOCH, J. R. *Dictionary, Practical, Theoretical and Historical, of Commerce and Commercial Navigation.* Ed. by Henry Vethake. 2 vols. London, 1850.

10 *Merchants' Magazine and Commercial Review.* 63 vols. New York, 1839-1870. (Title varies.)

11 SEAMAN, Ezra C. *Essays on the Progress of Nations.* New York, 1852. Repr New York, 1967.

12 TUCKER, George. *Progress of the United States.* New York, 1843.

13 United States Bureau of the Census. *Eighth Census, 1860, Mortality and Miscellaneous Statistics.* Washington, D.C., 1866. (For "Value of Real and Personal Estate," see 294-319.)

* * * * * * *

2. Other General Studies

14 BODE, Carl, ed. *American Life in the 1840's.* New York, 1967.†

15 BUDD, Edward C. "Factor Shares, 1850-1910," with comment by Edward F. Denison, and reply by Budd. See **34.5**, 365-406.

16 CALVERT, Monte A. *The Mechanical Engineer in America, 1830-1910: Professional Cultures in Conflict.* Baltimore, 1967.

17 DUPREE, A. Hunter. "Science and Technology," 117-122, with comment by Robert V. Bruce, 123-127. See **57.5**.

1 FISHLOW, Albert. "Levels of Nineteenth-Century American Investment in Education." *J Econ Hist,* XXV (1965), 418-436.

2 GALLMAN, Robert E. "Commodity Output, 1839-1899," with comment by Neal Potter, and reply by Gallman. See **34.5**, 13-71.

3 GALLMAN, Robert E. "Gross National Product in the United States, 1834-1909," with comment by Richard A. Easterlin. See **34.4**, 3-90.

4 GENOVESE, Eugene D. "Race and Class in Southern History: An Appraisal of the Work of Ulrich Bonnell Phillips." *Ag Hist,* XLI (1967), 345-358, with comments by David M. Potter, Kenneth M. Stampp, and Stanley Elkins, 359-372.

5 GILCHRIST, David T. and W. David LEWIS, eds. *Economic Change in The Civil War Era.* Proceedings of a Conference on American Institutional Change, 1850-1873, and the Impact of the Civil War held March 12-14, 1964. Greenville, Del., 1965.†

6 MILLER, Douglas T. *Jacksonian Aristocracy: Class and Democracy in New York, 1830-1860.* New York, 1967.

7 MORRISON, Rodney J. "Henry C. Carey and American Economic Development." *Explo Entrep Hist,* 2d ser, V (1968), 132-144.

8 NEVINS, Allan. *Abram S. Hewitt: With Some Account of Peter Cooper.* New York, 1935.

9 POTTER, J. "Atlantic Economy, 1815-1860: The USA and the Industrial Revolution in Britain," in *Studies in the Industries Revolution.* Ed. L. S. Presnell. London, 1960.

10 RATNER, Lorman. *Pre-Civil War Reform: The Variety of Principles and Programs.* Englewood Cliffs, N.J., 1967.†

11 ROSOVSKY, Henry ed. *Industrialization in Two Systems. Essays in Honor of Alexander Gerschenkron.* New York, 1966.

12 ROTHSTEIN, Morton. "The Ante-Bellum South as a Dual Economy: A Tentative Hypothesis." *Ag Hist,* XLI (1967), 373-382.

13 SCHLESINGER, Arthur M., Jr. *The Age of Jackson.* Boston, 1945.†

14 TAYLOR, George Rogers. "The National Economy before and after the Civil War." See **57.5**, 1-22.

3. *State and Regional Studies*

15 BEACH, M. Y. *Wealth and Wealthy Citizens of New York.* Published annually at New York from 1842 to 1855 with some variations in title.

16 HALL, James. *Notes on the Western States.* Philadelphia, 1838.

17 HALL, James. *Sketches of History Life and Manners in the West.* 2 vols. Philadelphia, 1835.

18 HALL, James. *Statistics of the West.* Cincinnati, 1837.

19 HALL, James. *The West: Its Commerce and Navigation.* Cincinnati, 1848.

20 HELPER, Hinton R. *The Impending Crisis of the South.* New York, 1860.†

1 KETTELL, Thomas P. *Southern Wealth and Northern Pofits, as Exhibited in Statistical Facts and Official Figures.* New York, 1860.
2 OLMSTED, Frederick L. *The Cotton Kingdom: A Traveller's Observations on Cotton and Slavery in the American Slave States.* 2 vols. New York, 1861. Repr New York, 1953.
3 OLMSTED, Frederick L. *A Journey in the Back Country in The Winter of 1853-4.* 2 vols. New York, 1860.
4 OLMSTED, Frederick L. *A Journey in the Seaboard Slave States, with Remarks on their Economy.* New York, 1856.
5 *Report of the Secretary of State Relative to Certain Branches of Industry.* Connecticut House of Representatives, Document No. 26, May Sess, 1839. Hartford, 1839.
6 *Statistical Information Relating to Certain Branches of Industry in Massachusetts, for the Year Ending June 1, 1855.* Boston, 1856.
7 *Statistical Information Relating to Certain Branches of Industry in Massachusetts, for the Year Ending May 1, 1865.* Boston, 1866.
8 *Statistical Tables: Exhibiting the Condition and Products of Certain Branches of Industry in Massachusetts, for the Year Ending April 1, 1837.* Boston, 1838.
9 *Statistics of the Condition and Products of Certain Branches of Industry in Massachusetts, for the Year Ending April 1, 1845.* Boston, 1846.
10 TYLER, Daniel P., comp. *Statistics of the Condition and Products of Certain Branches of Industry in Connecticut for the year Ending Oct 1, 1845.*

* * * * * * *

11 ARRINGTON, Leonard J. *Great Basin Kingdom: An Economic History of the Latter-Day Saints, 1830-1900.* Lincoln, Neb., 1967.†
12 CHRISTMAN, Henry. *Tin Horns and Calico.* New York, 1961.†
13 COLEMAN, Peter J. *The Transformation of Rhode Island, 1790-1860.* Providence, 1963.
14 EASTERLIN, Richard A. "Interregional Differences in Per Capita Income, Population, and Total Income, 1840-1950." See 34.5, 73-140.
15 LAMAR, Howard R. *The Far Southwest, 1846-1912.* New Haven, 1966.
16 LEIMAN, Melvin M. *Jacob N. Cardozo: Economic Thought in the Ante-Bellum South.* New York, 1966.
17 MEYER, John R. "Regional Economics: A Survey." *Am Econ Rev*, LIII (1963), 19-54. (Extensive references to regional and urban studies.)
18 MOORE, John H. "Economic Conditions in Mississippi on the Eve of the Civil War." *J Miss Hist*, XXII (1960), 167-178.
19 MORSE, Jarvis M. *A Neglected Period of Connecticut's History, 1818-1850.* New Haven, 1933. (See especially chap vi.)
20 RUSSELL, Robert R. *Economic Aspects of Southern Sectionalism, 1840-1861.* New York, 1924. Repr New York, 1960.
21 SMITH, Alfred G., Jr. *Economic Readjustment of an Old Cotton State: South Carolina, 1820-1860.* Columbia, S.C., 1958.

1 SYDNOR, Charles S. *The Development of Southern Sectionalism, 1819-1848.* Baton Rouge, 1948.

2 VAN DEUSEN, John G. *Economic Bases of Disunion in South Carolina.* Stud Hist Econ Pub Law (Colum). New York, 1928.

3 WILLIAMSON, Jeffrey G. "Regional Inequality and the Process of National Development, A Description of the Patterns." *Econ Dev Cult Change,* Suppl XIII (1965).

4 WILSON, Harold F. *The Hill Country of Northern New England.* New York, 1936.

4. Urban Studies

5 ADAMS, Nathaniel. *Annals of Portsmouth.* Portsmouth, N.H., 1825.

6 CIST, Charles. *Cincinnati in 1841: Its Early Annals and Future Prospects.* Cincinnati, 1841.

* * * * * * *

7 ALBION, Robert G. *The Rise of New York Port, [1815-1860].* New York, 1939.

8 BASSETT, T. D. Seymour. "A Case Study of Urban Impact on Rural Society: Vermont, 1840-1880." *Ag Hist,* XXX (1956), 28-34.

9 BASSETT, T. D. Seymour. "The Leading Villages of Vermont in 1840." *Vt Hist,* ns, XXVI (1958), 161-186.

10 BELCHER, W. W. *The Economic Rivalry between St. Louis and Chicago, 1850-1880.* Stud Hist Econ Pub Law (Colum). New York, 1947.

11 BOGLE, Victor M. "New Albany as a Commercial & Shipping Point, 1820." *Ind Mag Hist,* XLVIII (1952), 369-378.

12 BOGLE, Victor M. "New Albany: Mid-Nineteenth Century Economic Expansion." *Ind Mag Hist,* LIII (1957), 127-146.

13 BOGLE, Victor M. "New Albany's Attachment to the Ohio River." *Ind Mag Hist,* XLIX (1953), 249-266.

14 BOMAN, Martha. "A City of the Old South: Jackson, Mississippi, 1850-1860." *J Miss Hist,* XV (1953), 1-32.

15 COLE, Donald B. *Immigrant City: Lawrence, Massachusetts, 1845-1921.* Chapel Hill, 1963.

16 EDWARD, A. Wyatt, IV. "Rise of Industry in Ante-Bellum Petersburg." *Wm Mar Q,* 2d ser, XVII (1937), 1-36.

17 GREEN, Constance McLaughlin. *American Cities in the Growth of the Nation.* New York, 1957.†

18 GREEN, Constance McLaughlin. *Holyoke, Massachusetts.* New Haven, 1939.

19 HUSE, C. P. *The Financial History of Boston.* New York, 1916. Repr New York, 1967.

20 JORDAN, Weymouth T. *Ante-Bellum Alabama: Town and Country.* Tallahassee, Fla., 1957. (Concerns Mobile.)

1 LAMB, Robert K. "Entrepreneurship and Community Development," in *Explorations in Economics. Notes and Essays Contributed in Honor of F. W. Taussig.* New York, 1936, 526-534. (On Fall River and local entrepreneurship.)

2 MAC DONALD, Allan. "Lowell: A Commercial Utopia." *N Eng Q,* X (1937), 37-62.

3 PIERCE, Bessie L. *A History of Chicago.* 3 vols. New York, 1937, 1940, 1957.

4 SCHEIBER, Harry N. "Urban Rivary and Internal Improvements in the Old Northwest, 1820-1860." *Ohio Hist Q,* LXXI (1962), 227-239.

5 SHLAKMAN, Vera. *Economic History of a Factory Town: A Study of Chicopee, Massachusetts. Stud Hist* (Smith). Northampton, Mass., 1935.

6 SINCLAIR, Harold. *The Port of New Orleans.* New York, 1942.

7 SMITH, Alice E. *Millstone and Saw: The Origins of Neenah-Menasha.* Madison, 1966.

8 STAVISKY, Leonard P. "Industrialism in Ante-Bellum Charleston." *J Neg Hist,* XXXVI (1951), 302-322.

9 STILL, Bayrd. *Milwaukee, the History of a City.* Madison, 1948.

10 STILL, Bayrd. "Patterns of Mid-Ninteenth Century Urbanization in the Middle West." *Miss Val Hist Rev,* XXVIII (1941), 187-206.

11 TAYLOR, George Rogers. "American Urban Growth Preceding the Railway Age." *J Econ Hist,* XXVII (1967), 309-339.

12 VANCE, James E., Jr. "Housing the Worker: The Employment Linkage as a Force in Urban Structure." *Econ Geog,* XLII (1966), 294-325.

13 WARD, David. "The Industrial Revolution and the Emergence of Boston's Central Business District." *Econ Geog,* XLII (1966), 152-171.

14 WEATHERFORD, John W. "The Short Life of Manhattan, Ohio [1835-1848]." *Ohio Hist Q,* LXV (1956), 376-398.

15 WEBER, Adna F. *The Growth of Cities in the Nineteenth Century.* New York, 1899. Rev ed. Ithaca, 1963.†

16 WILLIAMSON, Jeffrey G. "Ante-Bellum Urbanization in the American Northeast." *J Econ Hist,* XXV (1965), 592-608.

17 WILLIAMSON, Jeffrey G. and Joseph A. SWANSON. "The Growth of Cities in the American Northeast, 1820-1870." *Explo Entrep Hist,* 2d ser, Suppl IV (1966).

5. Population, Immigration, and Migration

18 CHICKERING, Jesse. "Report of the Committee... and also a Comparative View of the Population of Boston in 1850...." Boston City Documents no 60, 1851.

19 SHATTUCK, Lemuel. *Report to the ... City Council. Census of Boston (1845) ... the Population, and their Means of Progress and Prosperity.* Boston, 1846.

* * * * * * *

1 ADAMS, William F. *Ireland and Irish Emigration to the New World from 1815 to the Famine.* New Haven, 1932.

2 ERNST, Robert. *Immigrant Life in New York City, 1825-1863.* New York, 1949.

3 GOODRICH, Carter, et al. *Migration and Economic Opportunity.* Philadelphia, 1936.

4 JORDAN, Terry G. *German Seed in Texas Soil: Immigrant Farmers in Nineteenth-Century Texas.* Austin, 1966.

5 LEE, Everett and Anne S. "Internal Migration Statistics for the United States." *J Am Stat Assn,* LV (1960), 664-697.

6 MAYER, Kurt B. and Sidney GOLDSTEIN. *Migration and Economic Development in Rhode Island.* Providence, 1958.

7 PAGE, Thomas W. "The Distribution of Immigrants in the United States before 1870." *J Pol Econ,* XX (1912), 676-694.

8 ROGERS, Tommy W. "The Great Population Exodus from South Carolina, 1850-1860." *S C Hist Mag,* LXVIII (1967), 14-21.

9 ROGERS, Tommy W. "Migration Pattern of Alabama's Population, 1850 and 1860." *Ala Hist Q,* XXVIII (1967), 45-50.

10 STILWELL, Lewis D. *Migration from Vermont.* Montpelier, 1948.

11 TAEUBER, Conrad and Irene B. *The Changing Population of the United States.* New York, 1958.

12 THOMAS, Brinley. *Migration and Economic Growth: A Study of Great Britain and the Atlantic Economy.* Cambridge, Eng., 1954. (Mostly on period after 1860.)

13 YASUBA, Yasukichi. *Birth Roles of the White Population of the United States, 1800-1860.* Baltimore, 1961.

6. Agriculture

14 HOUSE, Albert V. *Planter Management and Capitalism in Ante-Bellum Georgia: The Journal of Hugh Fraser Grant, Rice-Grower.* New York, 1954.

15 United States Bureau of the Census. *Eighth Census, 1860, Agriculture.* Washington, D.C., 1864.

16 WOODBURY, Levi. *A Report on the Cultivation, Manufacture and Foreign Trade of Cotton.* Exec Doc no 146, 24 Cong, 1 Sess, 1836. H of R ser no 289. Washington, D.C., 1836.

* * * * * *

17 BOGUE, Allan G. *From Prairie to Cornbelt, Farming on the Illinois and Iowa Prairies in the Nineteenth Century.* Chicago, 1963.

18 BOGUE, Margaret B. *Patterns from the Sod: Land Use and Tenure in the Grand Prairie, 1850-1900.* Springfield, Ill., 1959.

19 BRUCE, Kathleen. "A Fallacy: Virginian Agricultural Decline to 1860." *Ag Hist,* VI (1932), 3-13.

20 CARPENTER, Clifford E. "The Early Cattle Industry in Missouri." *Mo Hist Rev,* XLVII (1953), 201-215.

1 COLE, Arthur H. "Agricultural Crazes." *Am Econ Rev,* XVI (1926), 622-639.
2 COLMAN, Gould P. "Innovation and Diffusion in Agriculture." *Ag Hist,* XLII (1968), 173-187.
3 DANHOF, Clarence H. "The Fencing Problem in the Eighteen-Fifties." *Ag Hist,* XVIII (1944), 168-186.
4 DAVID, Paul A. "The Mechanization of Reaping in the Ante-Bellum Midwest." See 57.11, 3-39.
5 DONNELL, E. J. *Chronological and Statistical History of Cotton.* New York, 1872.
6 FIELDS, Emmett B. "The Agricultural Population of Virginia, 1850-1860." Dissertation, Vanderbilt U, 1953.
7 GALLMAN, Robert E. "A Note on the Patent Office Crop Estimates, 1841-1848." *J Econ Hist,* XXIII (1963), 185-195.
8 GATES, Paul W. *California Ranchos and Farms, 1846-1862.* Madison, 1967.
9 GATES, Paul W. "Hoosier Cattle Kings." *Ind Mag Hist,* XLIV (1948), 1-24.
10 GATES, Paul W. "Large-Scale Farming in Illinois, 1850 to 1870." *Ag Hist,* VI (1932), 14-25.
11 GENOVESE, Eugene D. "Livestock in the Slave Economy of the Old South—A Revised View." *Ag Hist,* XXXVI (1962), 143-149.
12 HAZEL, Joseph A. "The Geography of Negro Agricultural Slavery in Alabama, Florida and Mississippi." Dissertation, Columbia Univ, 1963.
13 HENLEIN, Paul C. "Early Cattle Ranges of the Ohio Valley." *Ag Hist,* XXXV (1961), 150-154.
14 JORDAN, Weymouth T. *Hugh Davis and His Alabama Plantation.* Montgomery, 1948.
15 KEMMERER, Donald L. "The Pre-Civil War South's Leading Crop, Corn." *Ag Hist,* XXIII (1949), 236-239.
16 LAMPARD, Eric E. *The Rise of the Dairy Industry in Wisconsin: A Study in Agricultural Change, 1820-1920.* Madison, 1963.
17 MOORE, John H. *Agriculture in Ante-Bellum Mississippi.* New York, 1958.
18 PARKER, William N. "The Slave Plantation in American Agriculture." See 4.17, 321-331.
19 PARKER, William N. and Judith L. V. KLEIN. "Productivity Growth in Grain Production in the United States, 1840-1860 and 1900-1910," with comment by Glen T. Barton. See 34.4, 523-582.
20 PRIMACK, M. L. "Land Clearing under Nineteenth-Century Techniques: Some Preliminary Calculations." *J Econ Hist,* XXII (1962), 484-497.
21 RANGE, Willard. *A Century of Georgia Agriculture, 1850-1950.* Athens, Ga., 1954.
22 ROGIN, Leo. *The Introduction of Farm Machinery in its Relation to the Productivity of Labor in Agriculture of the United States during the Nineteenth Century.* Pub Econ (Berk). Berkeley, 1931.

1 ROTHSTEIN, Morton. "The Ante-bellum Plantation as a Business Enterprise: A Review of Scarborough's *The Overseer." Explo Entrep Hist*, 2d ser, VI (1968), 128-133.

2 ROTHSTEIN, Morton. "The International Market for Agricultural Commodities, 1850-1873," with comments. See **57**.5, 73-82.

3 ROTHSTEIN, Morton. "Sugar and Secession: A New York Firm in Ante-Bellum Louisiana." *Explo Entrep Hist*, 2d ser, V (1968), 115-131.

4 SCARBOROUGH, W. K. *The Overseer: Plantation Management in the Old South*. Baton Rouge, 1966.

5 SITTERSON, J. Carlyle. "Financing and Marketing the Sugar Crop of the Old South." *J S Hist*, X (1944), 188-199.

6 THRONE, Mildred. "Southern Iowa Agriculture, 1833-1890: The Progress from Subsistence to Commercial Corn-Belt Farming." *Ag Hist*, XXIII (1949), 124-130.

7 WEAVER, Herbert. *Mississippi Farmers, 1850-1860*. Nashville, 1945.

8 WIK, Reynold M. *Steam Power on the American Farm*. Philadelphia, 1953.

7. *Public Land Policy, Land Speculation, and the Frontier*

9 ALLEN, Harry C. *Bush and Backwoods: A Comparison of the Frontier in Australia and the United States*. East Lansing, Mich., 1959.

10 BARRACLOUGH, Geoffrey. "Comment: The Seminal Character of Webb's Frontier Thesis." See **64**.19, 165-169.

11 BILLINGTON, Ray A. *The Far Western Frontier, 1830-1860*. New York, 1956.†

12 BILLINGTON, Ray A. "The Frontier in American Thought and Character." See **64**.19, 77-94.

13 BILLINGTON, Ray A. "The Origin of the Land Speculator as a Frontier Type." *Ag Hist*, XIX (1945), 204-212.

14 BILLINGTON, Ray A., ed. *The Frontier Thesis: Valid Interpretation of American History?* New York, 1966.† (Readings.)

15 BOGUE, Allan G. and Margaret B. " 'Profits' and the Frontier Land Speculator." *J Econ Hist*, XVII (1957), 1-24.

16 CARSTENSEN, Vernon, ed. *The Public Lands*. Madison, 1963.†

17 CHEYNEY, Edward P. *Anti-Rent Agitation in the State of New York, 1839-1846. Pol Econ Pub Law* (Penn). Philadelphia, 1887.

18 COLE, Arthur H. "Cyclical and Sectional Variations in the Sale of Public Lands, 1816-1860." *Rev Econ Stat*, IX (1927), 41-53.

19 CURTI, Merle E. *The Making of an American Community*. Palo Alto, Calif., 1959.

20 DANHOF, Clarence H. "Economic Validity of the Safety-Valve Doctrine." *J Econ Hist*, I (1941), 96-106.

21 DANHOF, Clarence H. "Farm-Making Costs and the 'Safety Valve,' 1850-1860." *J Pol Econ*, XLIX (1941), 317-359.

1 DE VOTO, Bernard. *Across the Wide Missouri.* Boston, 1947.†
2 DICK, Everett. *The Sod-House Frontier, 1854-1890.* New York, 1938.
3 DOWD, Douglas F. "A Comparative Analysis of Economic Development in the American West and South." *J Econ Hist,* XVI (1956), 558-574.
4 GARA, Larry. *Westernized Yankee: The Story of Cyrus Woodman.* Madison, 1956.
5 GATES, Paul W. "Charts of Public Land Sales and Entries." *J Econ Hist,* XXIV (1964), 22-27.
6 GATES, Paul W. *Fifty Million Acres: Conflicts over Kansas Land Policy, 1854-1890.* Ithaca, 1954.†
7 GATES, Paul W. *Frontier Landlords and Pioneer Tenants.* Ithaca, 1945. (Beginnings of large-scale farming in Illinois, 1835-1887.)
8 GATES, Paul W. "The Role of the Land Speculator in Western Development." *Penn Mag Hist Biog,* LXVI (1942), 314-333.
9 GERHARD, Dietrich. "The Frontier in Comparative View." *Comp Stud Soc Hist,* I (1959), 205-229.
10 GOODRICH, Carter and Sol DAVIDSON. "The Wage-Earner in the Westward Movement." *Pol Sci Q,* L (1935), 161-185.
11 HAWGOOD, John A. *America's Western Frontiers: The Story of the Explorers and Settlers who Opened the Trans-Mississippi West.* New York, 1967.
12 HOGAN, William R. "Comment: Fallacies in the Turner Thesis." See **64.19**, 125-131.
13 HURST, James Willard. *Law and Economic Growth: The Legal History of the Lumber Industry in Wisconsin, 1836-1915.* Cambridge, Mass., 1964.
14 ISE, John. "Pioneer Life in Western Kansas," in *Economics, Sociology and the Modern World. Essays in Honor of T. N. Carver.* Cambridge, Mass., 1935, 130-143.
15 JACOBS, Wilbur R., John W. CAUGHEY, and Joe B. FRANTZ. *Turner, Bolton, and Webb: Three Historians of the American Frontier.* Seattle, 1965.
16 LE DUC, Thomas. "The Disposal of the Public Domain on the Trans-Mississippi Plains." *Ag Hist,* XXIV (1950), 199-204.
17 LE DUC, Thomas. "Public Policy, Private Investment and Land Use in American Agriculture, 1825-1875." *Ag Hist,* XXXVII (1963), 3-9.
18 LENT, D. Geneva. *West of the Mountains: James Sinclair and the Hudson's Bay Company.* Seattle, 1963.
19 LEWIS, Archibald R. and Thomas F. MC GANN. *The New World Looks at its History: Proceedings of the Second International Congress of Historians of the United States and Mexico.* Austin, 1963. (Essays on the frontier in Mexico, Spain, and the United States.)
20 LITTLEFIELD, Henry M. "Has the Safety Valve come back to Life?" *Ag Hist,* XXXVIII (1964), 47-49.
21 LOKKEN, Roscoe L. *Iowa Public Land Disposal.* Iowa City, 1942.
22 LOWER, R. M. "Professor Webb and 'the Great Frontier' Thesis." See **64.19**, 142-154.

1 MC KITRICK, Reuben. *The Public Land System of Texas, 1823-1910.* Madison, 1918.

2 RIEGEL, Robert E. and Robert G. ATHEARN. *America Moves West.* 4th ed. New York, 1964.

3 ROBBINS, Roy M. "Horace Greeley: Land Reform and Unemployment, 1837-1862." *Ag Hist,* VII (1933), 18-41.

4 RODRIGUES, J. H. "Webb's Great Frontier and the Interpretation of Modern History." See **64**.19, 153-164.

5 SCHEIBER, Harry N. "State Policy and the Public Domain: The Ohio Canal Lands." *J Econ Hist,* XXV (1965), 86-113.

6 SEVERSON, Robert F., Jr., James F. NISS, and Richard D. WINKELMAN. "Mortgage Borrowing as a Frontier Developed: A Study of Mortgages in Champaign County, Illinois, 1836-1895." *J Econ Hist,* XXVI (1966), 147-168.

7 SHANNON, Fred A. "A Post Mortem on the Labor-Safety-Valve Theory." *Ag Hist,* XIX (1945), 31-37.

8 SHARP, Paul F. "Three Frontiers. Some Comparative Studies of Canadian, American, and Australian Settlement." *Pac Hist Rev,* XXIV (1955), 369-377.

9 STEVENS, Harry R. "Did Industrial Labor Influence Jacksonian Land Policy?" *Ind Mag Hist,* XLIII (1947), 159-167.

10 SWIERENGA, Robert P. "Land Speculator 'Profits' Reconsidered: Central Iowa as a Test Case." *J Econ Hist,* XXVI (1966), 1-28.

11 TAYLOR, George Rogers, ed. *The Turner Thesis Concerning the Role of the Frontier in American History.* Rev ed. Boston, 1956.†

12 TURNER, Frederick J. *The Frontier in American History.* New York, 1921.†

13 VON NARDROFF, Ellen. "The American Frontier as a Safety Valve: The Life, Death, Reincarnation and Justification of a Theory."*Ag Hist,* XXXVI (1962), 123-142.

14 WEBB, Walter P. *The Great Plains.* New York, 1931.†

15 WESTPHALL, Victor. *The Public Domain in New Mexico, 1854-1891.* Albuquerque, 1966.

16 WILLIAMS, Elgin. *The Animating Pursuits of Speculation: Land Traffic in the Annexation of Texas. Stud Hist Econ Pub Law* (Colum). New York, 1949.

17 WRIGHT, Benjamin F., Jr. "American Democracy and the Frontier." *Yale Rev,* XX (1930), 349-365.

18 WYMAN, Walker D. and Clifton B. KROEBER, eds. *The Frontier in Perspective.* Madison, 1957.†

19 ZAHLER, Helene S. *Eastern Workingmen and National Land Reform, 1829-1862.* New York, 1941.

8. Extractive Industry Other than Agriculture

20 BOWEN, Eli, ed. *The Coal Regions of Pennsylvania, being a General, Geological, Historical and Statistical Review of the Anthracite Coal Districts.* Pottsville, Pa., 1848.

1 United States Bureau of the Census. *Eighth Census, 1860. Mortality and Miscellaneous Statistics.* Washington, D.C., 1866. (For "The Fisheries," see 527-551.)

* * * * * * *

2 BEATON, Kendall. "Dr. Gesner's Kerosene: The Start of American Refining." *Bus Hist Rev,* XXIX (1955), 28-53.

3 BENEDICT, C. Harry. *Red Metal: The Calumet and Hecla Story.* Ann Arbor, 1952.

4 BRANCH, E. Douglas. *The Hunting of the Buffalo.* New York, 1929.

5 CRAMPTON, Charles G. "Gold Rushes and their Significance in the History of the Trans-Mississippi West." *Greater America; Essays in Honor of Herbert Eugene Bolton.* Berkeley, 1945, 519-533.

6 DURANT, Captain Edward W. "Lumbering and Steamboating on the St. Croix River." *Minn Hist Soc Coll,* X (1905), 645-675.

7 EAVENSON, Howard N. *The First Century and a Quarter of American Coal Industry.* Pittsburgh, 1942. (Useful, descriptive study with excellent maps showing coal fields and transportation routes.)

8 ELIASBERG, Vera F. "Some Aspects of Development in the Coal Mining Industry, 1839-1918," comments by Paul W. McGann and Harold J. Barnett. See **34.**4, 405-439.

9 FOLSOM, William H. C. "History of Lumbering in the St. Croix Valley, with Biographic Sketches." *Minn Hist Soc Coll,* IX (1901), 291-324.

10 GATES, William B. *Michigan Copper and Boston Dollars: An Economic History of the Michigan Copper Mining Industry.* Cambridge, Mass., 1951.

11 GREEVER, William S. *The Bonanza West: The Story of the Western Mining Rushes, 1848-1900.* Norman, Okla., 1963.

12 HERFINDAHL, Orris C. "Development of the Major Metal Mining Industries in the United States from 1839 to 1909," comment by Paul W. McGann. See **34.**4, 293-348.

13 HURST, James W. *Law and Economic Growth: The Legal History of the Lumber Industry in Wisconsin, 1836-1915.* Cambridge, Mass., 1964.

14 INGALLS, W. R. *Lead and Zinc in the United States.* New York, 1908.

15 LARSON, Agnes M. *History of the White Pine Industry in Minnesota.* Minneapolis, 1949.

16 MOMENT, David. "The Business of Whaling in America in the 1850's." *Bus Hist Rev,* XXXI (1957), 261-291.

17 MURDOCH, Angus. *Boom Copper: The Story of the First U.S. Mining Boom.* New York, 1943.

18 PAUL, Rodman W. *California Gold: THe Beginning of Mining in the Far West.* Cambridge, Mass., 1947.†

19 PAUL, Rodman W. *The Mining Frontiers of the Far West, 1848-1880.* New York, 1963.

20 RECTOR, William G. *Log Transportation in the Lake States Lumber Industry, 1840-1918.* Glendale, Calif., 1953.

21 RICE, Otis K. "Coal Mining in the Kanawha Valley to 1861." *J S Hist,* XXXI (1965), 393-416.

1 RICHTER, E. E. "The Copper-Mining Industry in the U.S., 1845-1925." *Q J Econ,* XLI (1927), 236-291.

2 STANCHFIELD, Daniel. "History of Pioneer Lumbering on the Upper Mississippi and its Tributaries, with Biographic Sketches." *Minn Hist Soc Coll,* IX (1901), 325-362.

3 STEPHENSON, Isaac. *Recollections of a Long Life, 1829-1915.* Chicago, 1915.

4 SUNDER, John E. *The Fur Trade on the Upper Missouri, 1840-1865.* Norman, Okla., 1965.

5 WOOD, R. G. *A History of Lumbering in Maine, 1820-1861.* Orono, Me., 1935.

6 WRIGHT, James E. *The Galena Lead District: Federal Policy and Practice, 1824-1847.* Madison, 1966.

7 YEARLEY, Clifton K., Jr. *Enterprise and Anthracite: Economics and Democracy in Schuylkill County, 1820-1875. Stud Hist Pol Sci* (Hop). Baltimore, 1961.

9. Transportation and Communication
A. GENERAL INCLUDING ROADS AND BRIDGES

8 ARMROYD, George. *A Connected View of the Whole Internal Navigation of the United States, Natural and Artificial; Present and Prospective.* Philadelphia, 1826.

9 GERSTNER, Franz A. *Die Innern Communication der Vereinigten Staaten von Nord America.* Vienna, 1842.

10 GILLESPIE, W. M. *A Manual of . . . Road-Making.* 5th ed. New York, 1852. (Includes material on plank roads, railroads. Largely technological.)

11 KINGSFORD, William. *History, Structure, and Statistics of Plank Roads, in the United States and Canada.* Philadelphia, 1851.

12 OWEN, Robert D. *A Brief Practical Treatise on the Construction and Management of Plank Roads.* New Albany, Ind., 1850.

13 TANNER, H. S. *A Description of the Canals and Rail Roads of the United States.* New York, 1840. (Contains a good map showing canals.)

* * * * * * *

14 BAUGHMAN, James P. "The Evolution of Rail-Water Systems of Transportation in the Gulf Southwest, 1836-1890." *J S Hist,* XXXIV (1968), 357-381.

15 BOGART, Ernest L. *Internal Improvement and State Debt in Ohio.* New York, 1924.

16 CLARK, W. H. *Railroads and Rivers.* Boston, 1939.

17 CROCKER, George G. *From the Stage-Coach to the Railroad Train and Street Car.* Boston, 1900.

18 DEARING, Charles L. *American Highway Policy.* Washington, D.C., 1941.

19 ESAREY, Logan. *Internal Improvements in Early Indiana.* Indianapolis, 1912.

1. FREDERICK, James. V. *Ben Holladay, the Stagecoach King.* Glendale, Calif., 1940.
2. HARDIN, Thomas L. "The National Road in Illinois." *J Ill State Hist Soc,* LX (1967), 5-22.
3. HARLOW, Alvin F. *Old Wires and New Waves: The History of the Telegraph, Telephone, and Wireless.* New York, 1936.
4. HOLMES, William F. "The New Castle and Frenchtown Turnpike and Railroad Company, 1809-1838: Part II, Canal Versus Railroad," and "Part III, From Horses to Locomotives." *Del Hist,* X (1962-1963), 152-180; 235-270.
5. HUNTER, Robert F. "The Turnpike Movement in Virginia, 1816-1860." *Va Mag Hist Biog,* LXIX (1961), 278-289.
6. JACKSON, Clayton. "The Internal Improvement Vetoes of Andrew Jackson." *Tenn Hist Q,* XXV (1966), 261-279.
7. JACKSON, W. Turrentine. *Wagon Roads West.* Berkeley, 1952.†
8. JORGENSEN, Charles J. "Transport Improvement and Economic Growth of the West, 1840-1860." Dissertation, U of Washington, 1962.
9. KIRKLAND, Edward C. *Men, Cities, and Transportation: A Study in New England History, 1820-1900.* 2 vols. Cambridge, Mass., 1948.
10. KOHN, David and Bess GLEN, eds. *Internal Improvements in South Carolina, 1817-1828.* Washington, D.C., 1938.
11. KRENKEL, John H. *Illinois Internal Improvements, 1818-1848.* Urbana, 1937. Repr Cedar Rapids, 1958.
12. LAMMONS, Frank B. "Operation Camel: An Experiment in Animal Transportation in Texas, 1857-1860." *S W Hist Q,* LXI (1957), 20-50.
13. LEBERGOTT, Stanley. "United States Transport Advance and Externalities," with "Discussion" by Harry N. Scheiber. *J Econ Hist,* XXVI (1966), 437-465.
14. MARTIN, William E. "Internal Improvements in Alabama." *Stud Hist Pol Sci* (Hop). Baltimore, 1902.
15. MOFFATT, Walter. "Transportation in Arkansas, 1819-1840." *Ark Hist Q,* XV (1956), 187-201.
16. PHILLIPS, Ulrich B. *A History of Transportation in the Eastern Cotton Belt to 1860.* New York, 1908.
17. RUBIN, Julius. *Canal or Railroad? Imitation and Innovation in the Response to the Erie Canal in Philadelphia, Baltimore and Boston.* Philadelphia, 1961.
18. SCHEIBER, Harry N. "Coach, Wagon and Motor-Truck Manufacture, 1813-1928: The Abbott-Downing Company of Concord." *Hist N H,* XX (1965), 3-25.
19. STEINMAN, David B. *The Builders of the Bridge: The Story of John Roebling and His Son.* New York, 1945.
20. TAYLOR, George Rogers. "The Beginnings of Mass Transportation in Urban America." *Smithsonian J Hist,* I (1966), No 2, 35-50; No 3, 31-54.

1 THOMPSON, Robert L. *Wiring a Continent: The History of the Telegraph Industry in the United States from 1832 to 1866*. Princeton, 1947.

2 WALKER, Henry P. *The Wagonmasters: High Plains Freighting from the Earliest Days of the Santa Fe Trail to 1880*. Norman, Okla., 1966.

B. WATER TRANSPORTATION

3 CAREY, Mathew. *Brief View of the System of Internal Improvements of the State of Pennsylvania*. Philadelphia, 1831.

4 United States Bureau of the Census. *Eighth Census, 1860, Mortality and Miscellaneous Statistics*. Washington, D.C., 1866. (For "Canal and River Improvements," see 335-336.)

5 ALBION, Robert G. *Square-Riggers on Schedule*. Princeton, 1938.

6 ANGAS, W. Mack. *Rivalry on the Atlantic, 1839-1939*. New York, 1939.

7 BISHOP, Avard L. *The State Works of Pennsylvania*. Tran Conn Acad Arts Sci. New Haven, 1908.

8 BOWEN, Frank C. *A Century of Atlantic Travel, 1830-1930*. Boston, 1930.

9 CHAPELLE, Howard I. *The Baltimore Clipper: Its Origin and Development*. Salem, Mass., 1930.

10 CHAPELLE, Howard I. *The History of American Sailing Ships*. New York, 1935.

11 CLARK, A. H. *The Clipper Ship Era*. New York, 1910.

12 CRANMER, H. Jerome. "Canal Investment, 1815-1860," with comment by Harvey H. Segal. See **34**.5, 547-570.

13 CUTLER, Carl C. *Greyhounds of the Sea: The Story of the American Clipper Ship*. New York, 1930.

14 DUNAWAY, Wayland F. *History of the James River and Kanawha Company*. Stud Hist Econ Pub Law (Colum). New York, 1922.

15 FISHLOW, Albert. Review of *Canals and American Economic Development* by Carter Goodrich and *Canal or Railroad?* by Julius Rubin. *J Econ Hist*, XIII (1963), 129-131.

16 GOODRICH, Carter, Julius RUBIN, Jerome H. CRANMER, and Harvey H. SEGAL. *Canals and American Economic Development*. New York, 1961.

17 GOULD, E. W. *Fifty Years on the Mississippi or History of River Navigation*. St. Louis, 1889.

18 GRAHAM, G. S. "The Ascendancy of the Sailing Ship, 1850-1885." *Econ Hist Rev*, 2d ser, IX (1956), 74-88.

19 HINSHAW, Clifford R., Jr. "North Carolina Canals before 1860." *N C Hist Rev*, XXV (1948), 1-57.

20 HUNTER, Louis C. *Steamboats on the Western Rivers*. Cambridge, Mass., 1949.

21 JACKSON, G. Gibbard. *The Ship under Steam*. New York, 1928.

22 JONES, Chester L. *The Economic History of the Anthracite-Tidewater Canals*. Ser Pol Econ Pub Law (Penn). Philadelphia, 1908.

1 KEILER, Hans. *American Shipping: Its History and Economic Conditions.* Jena, Germany, 1913.

2 LANE, Carl D. *American Paddle Steamboats.* New York, 1943.

3 MC CLELLAND, C. P. and C. C. HUNTINGTON. *History of the Ohio Canals: Their Construction, Cost, Use, and Partial Abandonment.* Columbus, 1905.

4 MAGINNIS, Arthur J. *The Atlantic Ferry, Its Ships, Men and Working.* New York, 1893.

5 MORRISON, John H. *History of American Steam Navigation.* New York, 1903.

6 MUSHAM, H. A. "Early Great Lakes Steamboats." "The First Propellers, 1841-1856." "The Chicago Line, 1838-1839." *Am Neptune,* XVII (1957), 89-104; XVIII (1958), 273-300.

7 PREBLE, George H. *A Chronological History of the Origin and Development of Steam Navigation, 1543-1882.* Philadelphia, 1883. 2d ed. Philadelphia, 1895.

8 PURDY, T. C. "Report on the Canals of the United States" in *Tenth Census of the United States, 1880.* Washington, D. C., 1883, IV, 725-764.

9 PURDY, T. C. "Report on Steam Navigation in the United States" in *Tenth Census of the United States, 1880.* Washington, D. C., 1883, IV, 653-724.

10 PUTNAM, James W. *The Illinois and Michigan Canal.* Chicago, 1918.

11 RANSOM, Roger L. "Canals and Development: A Discussion of the Issues." *Pap Proc Am Econ Rev,* LIV (1964), 365-376.

12 RANSOM, Roger L. "Interregional Canals and Economic Specialization in the Antebellum United States." *Explo Entrep Hist,* 2d ser, V (1967), 12-35.

13 RHOADS, Willard R. "The Pennsylvania Canal." *W Penn Hist Mag,* XLIII (1960), 203-238.

14 RUFFNER, Ernest H. *The Practice of the Improvement of the Non-Tidal Rivers of the United States.* New York, 1885.

15 RYDELL, Raymond A. "The California Clippers." *Pac Hist Rev,* XVIII (1949), 70-83.

16 SANDERLIN, Walter S. *The Great National Project: A History of the Chesapeake & Ohio Canal. Stud Hist Pol Sci* (Hop). Baltimore, 1946.

17 SCHEIBER, Harry N. "The Rate-Making Power of the State in the Canal Era: A Case Study." *Pol Sci Q,* LXXVII (1962), 397-413.

18 SHAW, Ronald E. *Erie Water West: A History of the Erie Canal, 1792-1854.* Lexington, Ky., 1966.

19 SHUMAN, Armin E. "Statistical Report of the Railroads of the United States" in *Tenth Census of the United States, 1880.* Washington, D. C., 1883, IV, 5-639. (For the historical summary see 299-375.)

20 THOMSON, David W. "The Great Steamboat Monopolies: Part I; The Mississippi," and "Part II, The Hudson." *Am Neptune,* VI (1956), 28-48; 270-280.

1 TRESCOTT, Paul B. "The Louisville and Portland Canal Company, 1825-1874." *Miss Val Hist Rev,* XLIV (1958), 686-708.

2 TYLER, D. B. *Steam Conquers the Atlantic.* New York, 1939.

3 WAGGONER, Madeline S. *The Long Haul West: The Great Canal Era, 1817-1850.* New York, 1958.

4 WARD, G. W. *The Early Development of the Chesapeake and Ohio Canal Project.* Stud Hist Pol Sci (Hop). Baltimore, 1899.

5 WHITFORD, Noble E. *History of the Canal System of the State of New York.* 2 vols. Albany, 1906.

C. RAILROADS

6 GRANT, E. B. *Boston Railways: Their Condition and Prospects.* Boston, 1856.

7 United States Bureau of the Census. *Eighth Census, 1860, Mortality and Miscellaneous Statistics.* Washington, D. C., 1866. (For "Progress of Railroads in the United States for the Decade of 1850-1860," see 323-334.)

* * * * * * *

8 ADLER, Dorothy R. "British Investment in American Railways, 1834-1898." Dissertation, Cambridge Univ, 1958.

9 ALEXANDER, E. P. *Iron Horses: American Locomotives, 1829-1900.* New York, 1941.

10 BAKER, G. P. *The Formation of the New England Railroad Systems.* Cambridge, Mass., 1937.

11 BAUGHMAN, Jampes P. *Charles Morgan and the Development of Southern Transportation.* Nashville, 1968.

12 BOGEN, Jules I. *The Anthracite Railroads.* New York, 1927.

13 BROWN, Cecil K. *A State Movement in Railroad Development.* Chapel Hill, 1928.

14 BURGESS, George H. and Miles C. KENNEDY. *Centennial History of the Pennsylvania Railroad Company, 1846-1946.* Philadelphia, 1949.

15 CARMAN, Harry J. *The Street Surface Railway Franchises of New York City.* New York, 1919.

16 CHANDLER, Alfred D., Jr. *Henry Varnum Poor.* Cambridge, Mass., 1956.

17 CHANDLER, Alfred D., Jr., ed. *The Railroads: The Nation's First Big Business.* New York, 1965. (Readings.)†

18 CLEVELAND, Frederick A. and Fred W. POWELL. *Railroad Promotion and Capitalization in the United States.* New York, 1909.

19 COOTNER, Paul H. "The Role of the Railroads in United States Economic Growth." *J Econ Hist,* XXIII (1963), 477-521, with discussion by Matthew Simon, 522-524, and Harry N. Scheiber, 525-528,

20 COTTERILL, R. S. "The Beginnings of Railroads in the Southwest." *Miss Val Hist Rev,* VIII (1922), 318-326.

21 COTTERILL, R. S. "Southern Railroads, 1850-1860." *Miss Val Hist Rev,* X, (1924), 396-405.

22 DERRICK, Samuel M. *Centennial History of the South Carolina Railroad.* Columbia, 1930.

1 FISHLOW, Albert. *American Railroads and the Ante-Bellum Economy.* Cambridge, Mass., 1965.

2 FISHLOW, Albert. "Productivity and Technological Change in the Railroad Sector, 1840-1910." See **34**.4, 583-646.

3 FOGEL, R. W. *Railroads and American Economic Growth.* See **5**.11.

4 GATES, Paul W. *The Illinois Central Railroad and its Colonization Work.* Har Econ Stud. Cambridge, Mass., 1934.

5 GATES, Paul W. "The Railroad Land-Grant Legend." *J Econ Hist,* XIV (1954), 143-146.

6 GLAAB, Charles N. *Kansas City and the Railroads.* Madison, 1962.

7 HARLOW, Alvin F. *Old Waybills: The Romance of the Express Companies.* New York, 1934.

8 HARLOW, Alvin F. *Steelways of New England.* New York, 1946.

9 HEATH, Milton. "Public Railroad Construction and the Development of Private Enterprise in the South before 1861." *J Econ Hist,* IX (1949), 40-53.

10 HENRY, Robert S. "The Railroad Land Grant Legend in American History Texts." *Miss Val Hist Rev,* XXXII (1945), 171-194.

11 HIDY, Ralph W. and Muriel E. "Anglo-American Merchant Bankers and the Railroads of the Old Northwest, 1848-1860." *Bus Hist Rev,* XXXIV (1960), 150-169.

12 HODGE, Charles L. "Economic Beginnings of the Boston and Albany Railroad, 1831-1867." See **8**.11, 446-469.

13 HUNGERFORD, Edward. *Men and Iron: The History of New York Central.* New York, 1938.

14 HUNGERFORD, Edward. *The Story of the Baltimore & Ohio Railroad, 1827-1927.* 2 vols. New York, 1928.

15 JENKS, Leland H. "Railroads as an Economic Force in American Development." *J Econ Hist,* IV (1944), 1-20.

16 JOHNSON, Arthur M. and Barry E. SUPPLE. *Boston Capitalists and Western Railroads: A Study in the Nineteenth-Century Railroad Investment Process.* Stud Bus Hist (Har). Cambridge, Mass., 1967.

17 KENNEDY, Charles J. "Commuter Services in the Boston Area, 1835-1860." *Bus Hist Rev,* XXXVI (1962), 153-170.

18 KENNEDY, Charles J. "The Eastern Railroad Company." *Bus Hist Rev,* XXXI (1957), 179-208.

19 KISTLER, Thelma M. "The Rise of Railroads in the Connecticut River Valley." *Stud Hist* (Smith). Northampton, Mass., 1938.

20 MC CLELLAND, Peter D. "Railroads, American Growth, and the New Economic History: A Critique." See **5**.18.

21 MOTT, Edward H. *Between the Ocean and the Lakes: The Story of the Erie.* New York, 1902.

22 MUIR, Andrew F. "Railroads Come to Houston, 1857-1861." *S W Hist Q,* LXIV (1960), 42-63.

23 OVERTON, Richard C. *Burlington Route: A History of the Burlington Lines.* New York, 1965.

1 OVERTON, Richard C. *Burlington West: A Colonization History of the Burlington Railroad.* Cambridge, Mass., 1941.

2 PAXSON, Frederic L. "The Railroads of the 'Old Northwest' before the Civil War." *Tran Wis Acad Sci Arts Letters,* XVII (1911), 243-274.

3 PIERCE, Harry H. *Railroads of New York: A Study of Government Aid, 1826-1875.* Cambridge, Mass., 1953.

4 PIXTON, John. *The Marietta and Cincinnati Railroad, 1845-1883.* University Park, Pa., 1966.

5 REED, Merl E. *New Orleans and the Railroads: The Struggle for Commercial Empire, 1830-1860.* Baton Rouge, 1966.

6 RIEGEL, Robert E. "Trans-Mississippi Railroads during the Fifties." *Miss Val Hist Rev,* X (1923), 153-172.

7 SALSBURY, Stephen. *The State, the Investor, and the Railroad: The Boston & Albany, 1825-1867.* Cambridge, Mass., 1967.

8 SCHOTT, Joseph L. *Rails Across Panama: The Story of the Building of the Panama Railroad, 1849-1855.* Indianapolis, 1967.

9 SCHUSLER, William K. "The Railroad Comes to Pittsburgh." *W Penn Hist Mag,* XLIII (1960), 251-266.

10 SEARS, Marian V. "Michigan Bureaucrat Promotes the States Economic Growth." *Explo Entrep Hist,* 2d ser, III (1966), 200-219.

11 STEVENS, Frank W. *The Beginnings of the New York Central Railroad.* New York, 1926.

12 STOVER, John F. *American Railroads.* Chicago, 1961.†

13 THOMPSON, Slason. *A Short History of American Railways, Covering Ten Decades.* New York, 1925.

14 TURNER, Charles W. "Virginia Railroad Development, 1845-1860." *Historian,* X (1947), 43-62.

15 WELLS, Henry. *Sketch of the Rise, Progress, and Present Condition of the Express System.* Albany, 1864.

16 WICKER, E. R. "Railroad Investment before the Civil War," with comments by George Rogers Taylor and Charles J. Kennedy. See **34**.5, 503-545.

10. Commerce

17 MILES, Pliny. *Advantages of Ocean Steam Navigation, Foreign and Coastwise, to the Commerce of Boston, and the Manufactures of New England.* Boston, 1857.

* * * * * * *

18 BENTON, Elbert J. *The Wabash Trade Route in the Development of the Old Northwest. Stud Hist Pol Sci* (Hop). Baltimore, 1903.

19 BOGART, Ernest L. "Early Canal Traffic and Railroad Competition in Ohio." *J Pol Econ,* XXI (1913), 56-70.

20 BULLOCK, Charles J., John H. WILLIAMS, and Rufus S. TUCKER. "The Balance of Trade of the United States." *Rev Econ Stat,* I (1919), 215-266.

1. CLARK, John G. "The Ante-Bellum Grain Trade of New Orleans." *Ag Hist,* XXXVIII (1964), 131-142.
2. CLARK, John G. *The Grain Trade in the Old Northwest.* Urbana, 1966.
3. CLARK, Thomas D. "Live Stock Trade between Kentucky and the South, 1840-1860." *Ky Hist Soc Reg,* XXVII (1929), 569-581.
4. COTTERILL, R. S. "Southern Railroads and Western Trade, 1840-1850." *Miss Val Hist Rev,* III (1917), 427-441.
5. ELLIS, David M. "Rivalry between the New York Central & the Erie Canal." *N Y Hist,* XXIX (1948), 268-300.
6. ELY, Roland T. "The Old Cuba Trade: Highlights and Case Studies of Cuban-American Interdependence during the Nineteenth Century." *Bus Hist Rev,* XXXVIII (1964), 456-478.
7. FISHLOW, Albert, "Ante-Bellum Interregional Trade Reconsidered." *Pap Proc Am Econ Rev,* LIV (1964), 352-364.
8. GLOVER, Frederick J. "Philadelphia Merchants and the Yorkshire Blanket Trade, 1820-1860." *Penn Hist,* XXVIII (1961), 121-141.
9. GOLDMAN, Henry H. "A Survey of Federal Escorts of the Santa Fe Trade, 1829-1843." *J W,* V (1966), 504-516.
10. GREGG, Josiah. *Commerce of the Prairies.* Ed. Max L. Moorehead. Norman, Okla., 1954.†
11. HILLIARD, Samuel B. "The Ante-Bellum Food Supply of Georgia, Alabama and Mississippi." Dissertation, U of Wis., 1966.
12. KOHLMEIER, Albert L. *The Old Northwest as the Keystone of the Arch of the American Federal Union: A Study in Commerce and Politics.* Bloomington, Ind., 1938.
13. MACESICH, George. "International Trade and U.S. Economic Development Revisited." *J Econ Hist,* XXI (1961), 384-385.
14. MASTERS, Donald C. *The Reciprocity Treaty of 1854.* New York, 1936.
15. NORTH, Douglass C. and Alan HESTON. "The Estimation of Shipping Earnings in Historical Studies of the Balance of Payments." *Can J Econ Pol Sci,* XXVI (1960), 265-276.
16. ROTHSTEIN, Morton. "Ante-Bellum Wheat and Cotton Exports." *Ag Hist,* XL (1966), 91-100.
17. SCHMIDT, Louis B. "Internal Commerce and the Development of National Economy before 1860." *J Pol Econ,* XLVII (1939), 798-822.
18. SCHMIDT, Louis B. "The Internal Grain Trade of the United States, 1850-1860." *Iowa J Hist Pol,* XVIII (1920), 94-124.
19. SMALLEY, Brian H. "Some Aspects of the Maine to San Francisco Trade, 1849-1852." *J W,* VI (1967), 593-603.
20. STERNS, Worthy P. "The Foreign Trade of the United States from 1820 to 1840." *J Pol Econ,* VIII (1900), 34-57.
21. SWITZLER, William F. *Report on the Internal Commerce of the United States.* U.S. Cong, House Ex Doc, 50th Cong, 1 Sess, No 6, Pt 2. Washington, D.C., 1888. Serial no 2552.

1. TEISER, Rugh and Catherine HARROUN. "Origin of Wells, Fargo & Company, 1841-1852." *Bull Bus Hist Soc,* XXII (1948), 70-83.
2. THOMPSON, R. T. "Transportation Combines and Pressure Politics in New Jersey, 1833-1836." *Proc N J Hist Soc,* LVII (1939), 1-15.
3. United States Treasury Department. *Statistics of the Foreign and Domestic Commerce of the United States.* Washington, D.C., 1864.
4. WAY, R. B. "The Commerce of the Lower Mississippi in the Period 1830-1860." *Proc Miss Val Hist Assn,* X (1918), 57-68.
5. WENDER, Herbert. *Southern Commercial Conventions, 1837-1860. Stud Hist Pol Sci* (Hop). Baltimore, 1930.
6. WILLIAMSON, Jeffrey G. *American Growth and the Balance of Payments, 1820-1913.* Chapel Hill, 1964.
7. WILLIAMSON, Jeffrey G. "International Trade and United States Economic Development, 1827-1843." *J Econ Hist,* XXI (1961), 372-383.
8. WILLIAMSON, Jeffrey G. "The Long Swing: Comparisons and Interactions between British and American Balance of Payments, 1820-1913." *J Econ Hist,* XXII (1962), 21-46.

11. Manufacturing

A. GENERAL INCLUDING TECHNOLOGY

9. FREEDLEY, Edwin T. *Philadelphia and Its Manufactures.* Philadelphia, 1859.
10. GREELEY, Horace, ed. *Art and Industry as Represented in the Exhibition at the Crystal Palace.* New York, 1853.
11. GREGG, William. *Essays on Domestic Industry.* 1st ed. Graniteville, S.C., 1845.
12. *McLane Report on Manufacturers, Documents Relative to Manufactures in the United States, House Document* No 308, 22d Cong, 1st Sess. 2 vols. Washington, D.C., 1833.
13. United States Bureau of the Census. *Eighth Census, 1860, Manufactures.* Washington, D.C., 1865.

* * * * * * *

14. BRAMSON, Roy T. *Highlights in the History of American Mass Production.* Detroit, 1945.
15. BURLINGAME, Roger. *Machines that Built America.* New York, 1953.†
16. CARMAN, Harry J. "The Rise of the Factory System." *History of the State of New York,* New York, 1934, VI, 191-245.
17. DAY, Clive. *The Rise of Manufacturing in Connecticut, 1820-1850.* Tercentenary Commission of the State of Connecticut, Vol XLIV. New Haven, 1935.
18. DUTTON, William S. *Du Pont: One Hundred and Forty Years.* 3d ed. New York, 1951.
19. FENICHEL, Ross M. "Growth and Diffusion of Power in Manufacturing, 1838-1919." See **34.4**, 443-478.

1 FISHER, Marvin. *Workshops in the Wilderness: The European Response to American Industrialization, 1830-1860.* New York, 1967.

2 GOLD, August B. "A History of Manufacturing in New York City, 1825-1840." Master's thesis, Columbia U, 1932.

3 GOTTLIEB, Manuel. "Building in Ohio between 1837 and 1914," with comment by Paul A. David, reply by Gottlieb. See **34**.4, 243-290.

4 GOTTLIEB, Manuel, "New Measures of Value of Nonfarm Building U.S.A. Annually, 1850-1939." *Rev Econ Stat,* XLVII (1965), 412-419.

5 GRIFFIN, Richard W. "The Augusta (Georgia) Manufacturing Company in Peace, War, and Reconstruction, 1847-1877." *Bus Hist Rev,* XXXII (1958), 60-73.

6 HABAKKUK, H. J. "Second Thoughts on American and British Technology in the Nineteenth-Century." *Business Archives and History,* III (1963), 187-194.

7 HUTCHINSON, William T. *Cyrus Hall McCormick: Seed-time, 1809-1856.* New York, 1930.

8 LINDEN, Fabian. "Repercussions of Manufacturing in the Ante-Bellum South." *N C Hist Rev,* XVII (1940), 313-331.

9 LIPPINCOTT, Isaac. *A History of Manufactures in the Ohio River to the Year 1860.* New York, 1914.

10 MERTON, Robert K. "Fluctuation in the Rate of Industrial Invention." *Q J Econ,* XLIX (1935), 454-474.

11 ROSENBERG, Nathan. "Technological Change in the Machine Tool Industry, 1840-1910." *J Econ Hist,* XXIII (1963), 414-443, with discussion by W. Paul Strassmann, 444-446.

12 SAWYER, John E. "The Social Basis of the American System of Manufacturing." *J Econ Hist,* XIV (1954), 361-379.

13 SCHURR, Sam H. *Energy in the American Economy, 1850-1975: An Economic Study of its History and Prospects.* Baltimore, 1960.

14 TEMIN, Peter. "Steam and Waterpower in the Early Nineteenth Century." *J Econ Hist,* XXVI (1966), 187-205.

15 WHITEHEAD, D. "American and British Technology in the Nineteenth Century." *Business Archives and History,* III (1963), 71-80.

16 WOODBURY, Robert S. *History of the Grinding Machine: A Historical Study in Tools and Precision Production.* Cambridge, Mass., 1959.

17 WOODBURY, Robert S. *History of the Milling Machine: A Study in Technical Development.* Cambridge, Mass., 1960.

18 WRIGHT, Carroll D. "Report of the Factory System of the United States." *Tenth Census of the United States, 1880.* Washington, D.C., 1883, II, 527-606.

19 ZEVIN, Robert B. "The Growth of Manufacturing in Early Nineteenth-Century New England." *J Econ Hist,* XXV (1965), 680-682.

B. INDUSTRY STUDIES

20 DUDLEY, J. G. *Cotton: A Paper on the Growth, Trade, and Manufacture of Cotton.* New York, 1853.

1. WHITWORTH, Joseph and George WALLIS. *The Industry of the United States in Machinery, Manufactures, and Useful and Ornamental Arts.* New York, 1854.

* * * * * * *

2. ARRINGTON, Leonard J. "Planning an Iron Industry for Utah, 1851-1858." *Huntington Lib Q,* XXI (1958), 237-260.

3. BEAME, Edmond M. "Rochester's Flour-Milling Industry in Pre-Canal Days." *Bus Hist Rev,* XXXI (1957), 209-225.

4. BINDER, Frederick M. "Gas Light (1816-1860)." *Penn Hist,* XX (1955), 359-373.

5. BLICKSILVER, Jack. *Cotton Manufacturing in the Southeast: An Historical Analysis.* Atlanta, 1959.

6. BOORSTIN, Daniel J. "The Balloon-Frame House" *The Americans: The National Experience.* New York, 1965, 148-152.

7. CLARK, Marcolm C. "The Birth of an Enterprise: Baldwin Locomotive, 1831-1842." *Penn Mag Hist Biog,* XC (1966), 423-444.

8. COCHRAN, Thomas C. *The Pabst Brewing Company.* New York, 1948.

9. COLE, Arthur H. and Harold F. WILLIAMSON. *The American Carpet Manufacture. Har Econ Stud.* Cambridge, Mass., 1941.

10. DAVIS, Lance E. and H. Louis STETTLER, III. "The New England Textile Industry, 1825-1860: Trends and Fluctuations," with comment by Paul F. McGouldrick, reply by Davis and Stettler. See **34.**4, 213-242.

11. DAVIS, Lance E. "The New England Textile Mills and the Capital Markets: A Study of Industrial Borrowing, 1840-1860." *J Econ Hist,* XX (1960), 1-30.

12. DEW, Charles B. *Ironmaker to the Confederacy: Joseph R. Anderson and the Tredegar Iron Works.* New Haven, 1966.

13. EWING, John S. and Nancy B. NORTON. *Broadlooms and Businessmen: A History of the Biglow-Sanford Carpet Company, 1825-1953. Stud Bus Hist* (Har). Cambridge, Mass., 1955.

14. FITCH, James M. *American Building: The Forces that Shape It.* Boston, 1948.

15. GIBB, George S. *The Whitesmiths of Taunton: A History of Reed & Barton, 1824-1943. Stud Bus Hist* (Har). Cambridge, Mass., 1943.

16. GIBSON, George H. "The Delaware Woolen Industry." *Del Hist,* XII (1966), 83-120.

17. GIBSON, George H. "Fullers, Carders, and Manufacturers of Woolen Goods in Delaware." *Del Hist,* XII (1966), 25-53.

18. GRIFFIN, Richard W. "Cotton Manufacture in Alabama to 1865." *Ala Hist Q,* XVIII (1956), 289-307.

19. GRIFFIN, Richard W. "The Origins of the Industrial Revolution in Georgia: Cotton Textiles, 1810-1865." *Ga Hist Q,* XLII (1958), 355-375.

20. GRIFFIN, Richard W. "Pro-Industrial Sentiment and Cotton Factories in Arkansas, 1820-1863." *Ark Hist Q,* XV (1956), 125-139.

21. GRIFFIN, Richard W. "The Textile Industry in Greene County, Georgia before 1860." *Ga Hist Q,* XLVIII (1964), 81-84.

1. HANSON, K. R. "New Jersey's First Anthracite Blast Furnace." *Proc N J Hist Soc,* LXXIX (1961), 111-117.
2. HUNTER, Louis C. "Factors in the Early Pittsburgh Iron Industry." See 8.11, 424-445.
3. HUNTER, Louis C. "Financial Problems of the Early Pittsburgh Iron Manufacturers." *J Econ Bus Hist,* II (1930), 520-544.
4. HUNTER, Louis C. "Influence of the Market upon Technique in the Iron Industry of Western Pennsylvania to 1860." *J Econ Bus Hist,* I (1929), 241-281.
5. KEITH, H. C. and C. R. HARTE. *The Early Iron Industry of Connecticut.* New Haven, 1935.
6. KNOWLTON, Evelyn H. *Pepperell's Progress: History of a Cotton Textile Company, 1844-1945. Stud Bus Hist* (Har). Cambridge, Mass., 1945.
7. LYON, Peter. "Isaac Singer and His Wonderful Sewing Machine." *Am Her,* IX (1958), 34-38, 103-109.
8. MC NAIR, J. B. *Simon Cameron's Adventure in Iron, 1837-1846.* Los Angeles, 1949.
9. MARBURG, Theodore. *Small Business in Brass Fabricating: The Smith and Griggs Manufacturing Company of Waterbury.* New York, 1956.
10. MITCHELL, Broadus. *The Rise of Cotton Mills in the South. Stud Hist Pol Sci* (Hop). Baltimore, 1921. Repr Magnolia, Mass., 1967.
11. MITCHELL, Broadus. *William Gregg, Factory Master of the Old South.* Chapel Hill, 1928.
12. MOORE, Charles W. *Timing a Century: History of the Waltham Watch Company. Stud Bus Hist* (Har). Cambridge, Mass., 1945.
13. MOORE, John H. "Mississippi's Ante-Bellum Textile Industry." *J Miss Hist,* XVI (1954), 81-98.
14. MORRIS, James A. *Woolen and Worsted Manufacturing in the Southern Piedmont.* Columbia, S.C., 1952.
15. NAVIN, Thomas R. *The Whitin Machine Works Since 1831: A Textile Machinery Company in an Industrial Village. Stud Bus Hist* (Har). Cambridge, Mass., 1950.
16. NORRIS, James D. "Business Longevity and the Frontier Iron Industry." *Papers Presented at the Annual Business History Conference.* Ed. J. Van Fenstermaker. Kent, Ohio, 1965, 31-38.
17. NORRIS, James D. *Frontier Iron: The Maramec Iron Works, 1826-1876.* Madison, 1964.
18. ROBINSON, Harriet H. *Loom and Spindle or Life Among the Early Mill Girls.* New York, 1898.
19. SMITH, Thomas R. *The Cotton Textile Industry of Fall River, Massachusetts, A Study of Industrial Location.* New York, 1944.
20. STANDARD, Diffee and Richard W. GRIFFIN. "The Cotton Textile Industry in Ante-Bellum North Carolina: Part II, An Era of Boom and Consolidation, 1830-1860." *N C Hist Rev,* XXXIV (1957), 131-164.
21. TEMIN, Peter. *Iron and Steel in Nineteenth-Century America.* Cambridge, Mass., 1964.
22. TEMIN, Peter. "A New Look at Hunter's Hypothesis about the Ante-Bellum Iron Industry." *Pap Proc Am Econ Rev,* LIV (1964), 344-351.

1 TYLER, D. B. *The American Clyde: A History of Iron and Steel Shipbuilding on the Delaware from 1840 to World War I.* Newark, Del., 1958.

12. Labor

A. GENERAL

2 BAILYN, Bernard. *Education in the Forming of American Society: Needs and Opportunities for Study.* Chapel Hill, 1960.†

3 BEZANSON, Anne. "Some Historical Aspects of Labor Turnover." See 8.11, 692-708.

4 CARLTON, Frank T. *Economic Influences upon Educational Progress in the United States, 1820-1850. Econ Pol Sci Ser* (Wis). Madison, 1908.

5 CHIU, Ping. *Chinese Labor in California, 1850-1880: An Economic Study.* Madison, 1963.

6 COMMONS, John R. *Labor Movement, 1840-1860.* See 7.1, vols 7-8.

7 COMMONS, John R. and Helen L. SUMNER. *Labor Movement, 1820-1840.* See 7.1, vols 5-6.

8 DRUMMOND, Ian M. "Labor Scarcity and the Problem of American Industrial Efficiency in the 1850's: A Comment." *J Econ Hist,* XXVII (1967), 383-390.

9 FARNAM, H. W. *Chapters in the History of Social Legislation in the United States to 1860.* Washington, D.C., 1938.

10 FISHLOW, Albert. "The Common School Revival: Fact or Fancy." See 57.11, 40-67.

11 GINGER, Ray. "Labor in a Massachusetts Cotton Mill, 1853-1860." *Bus Hist Rev,* XXVIII (1954), 67-91.

12 HARTZ, Louis. "Seth Luther: Working Class Rebel." *N Eng Q,* XIII (1940), 401-418.

13 LITWACK, Leon F. *North of Slavery: The Negro in the Free States, 1790-1860.* Chicago, 1961.†

14 MC BEE, Alice E. *From Utopea to Florence: The Story of a Transcendentalist Community in Northampton, Massachusetts, 1830-1852. Stud Hist* (Smith). Northampton, Mass., 1947.

15 MORRIS, Richard B. "Labor Controls in Maryland in the Nineteenth Century." *J S Hist,* XIV (1948), 385-400.

16 PELLING, Henry. *American Labor.* Chicago, 1960.†

17 PESSEN, Edward. *Most Uncommon Jacksonians: The Radical Leaders of the Early Labor Movement.* Albany, 1968.

18 PRIMACK, M. L. "Farm Construction as a Use of Farm Labor in the United States, 1850-1910." *J Econ Hist,* XXV (1965), 114-125.

19 RANDALL, Edwin T. "Imprisonment for Debt in America: Fact and Fiction." *Miss Val Hist Rev,* XXXIX (1952), 89-102.

1 ROZWENC, Edwin C. *Cooperatives Come to America.* Mount Vernon, Iowa, 1941.

2 SULLIVAN, William A. "The Industrial Revolution and the Factory Operative in Pennsylvania." *Penn Mag Hist Biog,* LXXVIII (1954), 476-494.

3 TEMIN, Peter. "Labor Scarcity and the Problem of American Industrial Efficiency in the 1850's." *J Econ Hist,* XXVI (1966), 277-298.

4 WARE, Norman. *The Industrial Worker, 1840-1860.* Boston, 1924.†

5 WHELPTON, P. K. "Occupational Groups in the United States, 1820-1920." *J Am Stat Assn,* XXI (1926), 335-343.

6 YEARLEY, Clifton K., Jr. *Britons in American Labor: A History of the Influence of the United Kingdom Immigrants on American Labor, 1820-1914.* Stud Hist Pol Sci (Hop). Baltimore, 1957.

B. FREE LABOR: LIVING AND WORKING CONDITIONS

7 ARKY, Louis. "The Mechanics' Union of Trade Associations and the Formation of the Philadelphia Workingmen's Movement."*Penn Mag Hist Biog,* LXXVI (1952), 142-176.

8 BERNSTEIN, Leonard. "The Working People of Philadelphia from Colonial Times to the General Strike of 1835." *Penn Mag Hist Biog,* LXXIV (1950), 322-339.

9 BOWER, Robert T. "Note on 'Did Labor Support Jackson?: The Boston Story.'" *Pol Sci Q,* LXV (1950), 441-444.

10 BREMNER, Robert H. *From the Depths: The Discovery of Poverty in the United States.* New York, 1956.†

11 CALVERT, Monte A. "The Allegheny City Cotton Mill Riot of 1848." *W Penn Hist Mag,* XLVI (1963), 97-133.

12 DARLING, Arthur B. "The Workingmen's Party in Massachusetts, 1833-1834." *Am Hist Rev,* XXIX (1923), 81-86.

13 DORFMAN, Joseph. "The Jackson Wage-Earner Thesis." *Am Hist Rev,* LIV (1949), 296-306.

14 GRIFFIN, Richard W. "Poor White Laborers in Southern Cotton Factories." *S C Hist Mag,* LXI (1960), 26-40.

15 HOFSTADTER, Richard. "William Leggett, Spokesman of Jacksonian Democracy." *Pol Sci Q,* LVIII (1943), 581-594.

16 HUGINS, Walter. *Jacksonian Democracy and the Working Class: A Study of the New York Workingmen's Movement, 1829-1837.* Stanford, Calif., 1960.†

17 JACKSON, Sidney L. "Labor, Education, and Politics in the 1830's." *Penn Mag Hist Biog,* LXVI (1942), 279-293.

18 JOSEPHSON, Hannah. *The Golden Threads: New England's Mill Girls and Magnates.* New York, 1949.

19 KLEBANER, Benjamin J. "Employment of Paupers at Philadelphia's Almshouse before 1861." *Penn Hist,* XXIV (1957), 137-147.

1 LAYER, Robert G. *Earnings of Cotton Mill Operatives, 1825-1914*. Cambridge, Mass., 1955.†

2 MARTIN, Edgar W. *The Standard of Living in 1860*. Chicago, 1942.

3 MORRIS, Richard B. "Andrew Jackson, Strike-breaker." *Am Hist Rev*, LV (1949), 54-68.

4 NADWORNY, Milton J. "New Jersey Workingmen and the Jacksonians." *Proc N J Hist Soc*, LXVII (1949), 185-198.

5 NOLEN, Russell M. "The Labor Movement in St. Louis Prior to the Civil War." *Mo Hist Rev*, XXXIV (1939), 18-37.

6 PERSONS, Charles E. "Early History of Factory Legislation in Massachusetts," in *Labor Laws and Their Enforcement*. Ed. by Susan M. Kingsbury. New York, 1911, 3-142.

7 PESSEN, Edward. "Did Labor Support Jackson: The Boston Story." *Pol Sci Q*, LXIV (1949), 262-274.

8 PESSEN, Edward. "The Ideology of Stephen Simpson, Upperclass Champion of the Early Philadelphia Workingmen's Movement." *Penn Hist*, XXII (1955), 328-340.

9 PESSEN, Edward. "Thomas Skidmore (1790-1832), Agrarian Reformer in the Early American Labor Movement." *N Y Hist*, XXXV (1954), 280-296.

10 PESSEN, Edward. "The Workingmen's Movement of the Jacksonian Era." *Miss Val Hist Rev*, XLIII (1956), 428-443.

11 PESSEN, Edward. "The Working Men's Party Revisited." *Labor Hist*, IV (1963), 203-226.

12 ROSENBERG, Nathan. "Anglo-American Wage Differences in the 1820's." *J Econ Hist*, XXVII (1967), 221-229.

13 SMITH, Walter B. "Wage Rates on the Erie Canal, 1828-1881." *J Econ Hist*, XXIII (1963), 298-311.

14 SULLIVAN, William A. "Did Labor Support Andrew Jackson?" *Pol Sci Q*, LXII (1947), 569-580.

15 SULLIVAN, William A. "Philadelphia Labor during the Jackson Era." *Penn Hist*, XV (1948), 305-320.

16 ULMAN, Lloyd. *The Rise of the National Trade Union*. Cambridge, Mass., 1955.

C. SLAVERY

17 BANCROFT, Frederic. *Slave-Trading in the Old South*. Baltimore, 1931.

18 ELKINS, Stanley. *Slavery: A Problem in American Institutional and Intellectual Life*. Chicago, 1959.†

19 ENGERMAN, Stanley L. "The Effects of Slavery upon the Southern Economy: A Review of the Recent Debate." *Explo Entrep Hist*, 2d ser, IV (1967), 71-97.

20 FISCHBAUM, Marvin and Julius RUBIN. "Slavery and the Economic Development of the American South." *Explo Entrep Hist*, 2d ser, VI (1968), 116-127.

1 FONER, Philip S. *Business and Slavery*. Chapel Hill, 1941.
2 GENOVESE, Eugene D. "The Medical and Insurance Costs of Slaveholding in the Cotton Belt." *J Neg Hist*, XLV (1960), 141-155.
3 GENOVESE, Eugene D. "The Significance of the Slave Plantation for Southern Economic Development." *J S Hist*, XXVIII (1962), 422-437.
4 LINDEN, Fabian. "Economic Democracy in the Slave South: An Appraisal of Some Recent Views." *J Neg Hist*, XXXI (1946), 140-189.
5 MENN, J. K. *The Large Slaveholders of Louisiana, 1860*. New Orleans, 1964.
6 MORROW, Ralph E. "The Proslavery Argument Revisited." *Miss Val Hist Rev*, XLVIII (1961), 79-94.
7 PHILLIPS, Ulrich B. "The Economic Cost of Slaveholding in the Cotton Belt." *Pol Sci Q*, XX (1905), 257-275.
8 PHILLIPS, Ulrich B. *Life and Labor in the Old South*. Boston, 1929.†
9 ROZWENC, Edwin C., ed. *Slavery as a Cause of the Civil War*. Rev ed. Boston, 1963.† (Readings.)
10 RUSSELL, Robert R. "The General Effects of Slavery upon Southern Economic Progress." *J S Hist*, IV (1938), 35-54.
11 SARAYDAR, Edward. "A Note on the Profitability of Ante-Bellum Slavery." *S Econ J*, XXX (1964), 325-332.
12 SELLERS, J. B. *Slavery in Alabama*. University, Ala., 1950.
13 STAMPP, Kenneth M. *The Peculiar Institution: Slavery in the Ante-Bellum South*. New York, 1956.
14 SUTCH, Richard. "The Profitability of Ante-Bellum Slavery Revisited." *S Econ J*, XXXI (1965), 365-377, with reply by Edward Saraydar, 377-383.
15 SYDNOR, Charles S. *Slavery in Mississippi*. Baton Rouge, 1966.
16 TAYLOR, Joe G. *Negro Slavery in Louisiana*. Baton Rouge, 1963.
17 TAYLOR, Paul S. "Plantation Laborer before the Civil War." *Ag Hist*, XXVIII (1954), 1-21.
18 WADE, Richard C. *Slavery in the Cities*. New York, 1964.
19 WOODMAN, Harold D. "The Profitability of Slavery: A Historical Perennial." *J S Hist*, XXIX (1963), 303-325.

13. Public Finance

20 BOURNE, Edward G. *The History of the Surplus Revenue of 1837*. New York, 1885.
21 DAVIS, Lance E. and John LEGLER. "The Government in the American Economy, 1815-1902: A Quantitative Study." *J Econ Hist*, XXV (1965), 514-552.
22 DECKER, Leslie E. *Railroads, Land, and Politics: The Taxation of Railroad Land Grants, 1864-1897*. Providence, 1964.
23 KINLEY, David. *The History, Organization and Influence of the Independent Treasury of the United States*. New York, 1893.

1 KINLEY, David. *The Independent Treasury of the United States and Its Relations to the Banks of the Country.* Washington, D.C., 1910.

2 MC GRANE, Reginald C. *Foreign Bondholders and American State Debts.* New York, 1935.

3 PATTERSON, Robert T. "Government Finance on the Eve of the Civil War." *J Econ Hist,* XII (1952), 35-44.

4 THOMPSON, James H. "The Financial History of Pittsburgh: The Early Period 1816-1865." *W Penn Hist Mag,* XXXIII (1950), 43-64.

5 TIMBERLAKE, Richard H., Jr. "Ideological Factors in Specie Resumption and Treasury Policy." *J Econ Hist,* XXIV (1964), 29-52.

6 TIMBERLAKE, Richard H., Jr. "The Independent Treasury and Monetary Policy before the Civil War." *S Econ J,* XXVII (1960), 92-103.

7 TIMBERLAKE, Richard H., Jr. "The Specie Circular and Sales of Public Lands: A Comment." *J Econ Hist,* XXV (1965), 414-416.

14. Money and Banking

8 COLWELL, Stephen. *The Ways and Means of Payment.* Philadelphia, 1859.

9 GALLATIN, Albert. *Considerations on the Currency and Banking System of the United States.* Philadelphia, 1831.

10 GALLATIN, Albert. *Suggestions on the Banks and Currency.* New York, 1841.

11 GOUGE, William M., ed. *The Journal of Banking.* Philadelphia, 1842.

12 GOUGE, William M. *A Short History of Paper-Money and Banking in the United States.* New York, 1835.

13 RAGUET, Condy. *A Treatise on Currency and Banking.* 2d ed. Philadelphia, 1840.

* * * * * *

14 BROWN, K. L. "Stephen Girard, Promoter of the Second Bank of the United States." *J Econ Hist,* II (1942), 125-148.

15 CATTERALL, Ralph C. *The Second Bank of the United States.* Chicago, 1903.

16 DEWEY, Davis R. *The Second Bank of the United States.* Washington, D.C., 1910.

17 DILLISTIN, W. H. *Bank Note Reporters and Counterfeit Detectors, 1826-1866.* New York, 1949.

18 DUNNE, Gerald T. *Monetary Decisions of the Supreme Court.* New Brunswick, 1960.

19 GATELL, Frank O. *The Jacksonians and the Money Power.* Chicago, 1968.

20 GATELL, Frank O. "Secretary Taney and the Baltimore Pets: A Study in Banking and Politics." *Bus Hist Rev,* XXXIX (1965), 205-227.

1. GATELL, Frank O. "Spoils of the Bank War: Political Bias in the Selection of Pet Banks." *Am Hist Rev,* LXX (1964), 35-58.
2. GOLEMBE, Carter H. "State Banks and the Economic Development of the West, 1830-1844." Dissertation, Columbia Univ, 1952.
3. GOVAN, Thomas P. *Nicholas Biddle, Nationalist and Public Banker, 1786-1844.* Chicago, 1959.
4. HAMMOND, Bray. "Jackson, Biddle, and the Bank of the United States." *J Econ Hist,* VII (1947), 1-23.
5. HAMMOND, Bray. "Review of Schlesinger's *The Age of Jackson.*" *J Econ Hist,* VI (1946), 79-84.
6. HEDGES, Joseph E. *Commercial Banking and the Stock Market before 1863. Stud Hist Pol Sci* (Hop). Baltimore, 1938.
7. HIDY, Ralph W. "The House of Baring and the Second Bank of the United States, 1826-1836," *Penn Mag Hist Biog,* LXVIII (1944), 269-285.
8. JAMES, F. Cyril. *The Growth of Chicago Banks.* 2 vols. New York, 1938.
9. LA FORCE, J. C. "Gresham's Law and the Suffolk System: A Misapplied Epigram." *Bus Hist Rev,* XL (1966), 149-189.
10. MACESICH, George. "Counterfeit Detectors and Pre-1860 Monetary Statistics." *J S Hist,* XXVII (1961), 229-232.
11. MACESICH, George. "Sources of Monetary Disturbances in the United States, 1834-1845." *J Econ Hist,* XX (1960), 407-434.
12. NEU, Irene D. "J. B. Moussier and the Property Banks of Louisiana." *Bus Hist Rev,* XXXV (1961), 550-557.
13. PAYNE, Peter L. and Lance E. DAVIS. *The Savings Bank of Baltimore, 1818-1866.* Baltimore, 1956.
14. PLOUS, Harold J. "Jackson, the Bank War, and Liberalism." *S W Soc Sci Q,* XXXVIII (1957), 99-110.
15. REMINI, Robert V. *Andrew Jackson and the Bank War.* New York, 1967.
16. SCHEIBER, Harry N. "The Commercial Bank of Lake Erie, 1831-1843." *Bus Hist Rev,* XL (1966), 47-65.
17. SCHEIBER, Harry N. "The Pet Banks in Jacksonian Politics and Finance, 1833-1841." *J Econ Hist,* XXIII (1963), 196-214.
18. SCHUR, Leon M. "The Second Bank of the United States and the Inflation after the War of 1812." *J Pol Econ,* LXVIII (1960), 118-134.
19. SCROGGS, William O. "Pioneer Banking in Alabama." See 8.11, 402-423.
20. SELLERS, Charles G., Jr. "Banking and Politics in Jackson's Tennessee, 1817-1827." *Miss Val Hist Rev,* XLI (1954), 61-84.
21. SMITH, Alice E. *George Smith's Money: A Scottish Investor in America.* Madison, 1966.
22. SMITH, Walter B. *Economic Aspects of the Second Bank of the United States.* Cambridge, Mass., 1953.
23. SWISHER, C. B. *Roger B. Taney.* New York, 1935. (Defends Jackson's position on the Second Bank.)
24. TIMBERLAKE, Richard H., Jr. "The Specie Standard and Central Banking in the U.S. before 1860." *J Econ Hist,* XXI (1961), 318-341.

1 WALTERS, Raymond, Jr. "The Origins of the Second Bank of the United States." *J Pol Econ,* LIII (1945), 115-131.

2 WARBURTON, Clark. "Variations in Economic Growth and Banking Developments in the United States from 1835-1885." *J Econ Hist,* XVIII (1958), 283-297.

3 WILBURN, Jean A. *Biddle's Bank, the Crucial Years.* New York, 1967.

4 WILLETT, Thomas D. "International Specie Flows and American Monetary Stability, 1834-1860." *J Econ Hist,* XXVIII (1968), 28-49.

5 WRIGHT, David M. "Langdon Cheves and Nicholas Biddle: New Data for a New Interpretation." *J Econ Hist,* XIII (1953), 305-319.

15. Prices and Business Conditions

6 BALDWIN, Joseph G. *The Flush Times of Alabama and Mississippi: A Series of Sketches.* New York, 1853.

7 GATELL, Frank O. "Sober Second Thoughts on Van Buren, the Albany Regency, and the Wall Street Conspiracy." *J Econ Hist,* LIII (1966), 19-40.

8 HABAKKUK, H. J. "Fluctuations in House-Building in Britain and the United States in the Nineteenth Century." *J Econ Hist,* XXII (1962), 198-230.

9 HOOVER, Ethel D. "Retail Prices after 1850," with comment by John W. Kendrick. See **34**.5, 141-190.

10 HUGHES, J. R. T. and Nathan ROSENBERG. "The United States Business Cycle before 1860: Some Problems of Interpretation." *Econ Hist Rev,* 2d ser, XV (1963), 476-493.

11 HUTCHINSON, A. E. "Philadelphia and the Panic of 1857." *Penn Hist,* III (1936), 182-194.

12 MC GRANE, Reginald C. *The Panic of 1837: Some Financial Problems of the Jacksonian Era.* Chicago, 1924.†

13 MATTHEWS, R. C. O. *A Study in Trade Cycle History: Economic Fluctuations in Great Britain, 1833-1842.* Cambridge, Eng., 1954. (Stresses the importance of British-United States relationships.)

14 REZNECK, Samuel. "The Influence of Depression upon American Opinion, 1857-1859." *J Econ Hist,* II (1942), 1-23.

15 REZNECK, Samuel. "The Social History of an American Depression, 1837-1843." *Am Hist Rev,* XL (1935), 662-687.

16 SCHUMPETER, J. A. *Business Cycles.* 2 vols. New York, 1939.

17 SCHWARTZ, Carol H. "Retail Trade Development in New York State in the 19th Century with Special Reference to the Country Store." Dissertation, Columbia U, 1963.

18 TEMIN, Peter. "The Causes of Cotton-Price Fluctuations in the 1830's." *Rev Econ Stat,* XLIX (1967), 463-470.

19 VAN VLECK, George W. *The Panic of 1857.* New York, 1943.

16. Capital, Corporate Securities, and Insurance

1 CHANDLER, Alfred D., Jr. "Patterns of American Railroad Finance, 1830-1850." *Bus Hist Rev,* XXVIII (1954), 248-263.

2 CLOUGH, Shepard B. *A Century of American Life Insurance: A History of the Mutual Life Insurance Company of New York, 1843-1943.* New York, 1946.

3 COLE, Arthur H. and Edwin FRICKEY. "The Course of Stock Prices, 1825-1866." *Rev Econ Stat,* X (1928), 117-139.

4 COONEY, E. W. "Capital Exports and Investment in Building in Britain and in the U.S.A., 1856-1914." *Economica,* ns, XVI (1949), 347-354.

5 DAVIS, Lance E. "The Capital Markets and Industrial Concentration: The U.S. and U.K., A Comparative Study." *Econ Hist Rev,* 2d ser, XIX (1966), 255-272.

6 DAVIS, Lance E. "Sources of Industrial Finance: The American Textile Industry: A Case Study." *Explo Entrep Hist,* IX (1957), 189-203.

7 DAVIS, Lance E. "Stock Ownership in the Early New England Textile Industry." *Bus Hist Rev,* XXXII (1958), 204-222.

8 EVANS, G. H., Jr. "The Early History of Preferred Stock in The United States." *Am Econ Rev,* XIX (1929), 43-58.

9 GREEF, Albert O. *The Commercial Paper House in the United States.* Har Econ Stud. Cambridge, Mass., 1938.

10 HEUBNER, Solomon. "History of Marine Insurance" *Property Insurance.* Ed. Lester Zartman. New Haven, 1914, 1-38.

11 HOMER, Sidney. *A History of Interest Rates.* New Brunswick, 1963. (For the U.S. in the 18th and 19th centuries see chap xvi.)

12 JAMES, Marquis. *The Metropolitan Life: A Study in Business Growth.* New York, 1947.

13 JENKS, Leland H. *The Migration of British Capital to 1875.* New York, 1927.

14 LYNN, Robert A. "Installment Credit before 1870." *Bus Hist Rev,* XXXI (1957), 414-424.

15 MYERS, Margaret G. *The New York Money Market.* Vol I, pt 1. New York, 1931.

16 NORTH, Douglass C. "International Capital Flows and the Development of the American West." *J Econ Hist,* XVI (1956), 493-505.

17 OLSEN, Bernard M. "The Origin of Capital for Early Indiana Manufacturing." Dissertation, Univ of Chicago, 1954.

18 PIERCE, Harry H. "Foreign Investment in American Enterprise," with comments. See 57.5, 41-61.

19 PRIMACK, M. L. "Farm Capital Formation as a Use of Farm Labor in the United States, 1850-1910." *J Econ Hist,* XXVI (1966), 348-362.

17. Business Organization and Marketing

1 HUNT, Freeman. *Lives of American Merchants.* 2 vols. New York, 1858.

* * * * * * *

2 ARRINGTON, Leonard J. *Oderville, Utah: A Pioneer Mormon Experiment in Economic Organization.* Salt Lake City, 1954.

3 ATHERTON, L. E. "Business Techniques in the Sante Fe Trail." *Mo Hist Rev,* XXXIV (1940), 335-341.

4 ATHERTON, L. E. *Main Street on the Middle Border.* Bloomington, Ind., 1954.†

5 ATHERTON, L. E. *The Pioneer Merchant in Mid-America. Stud* (Mo). Columbia, Mo., 1939.

6 BERRY, Thomas. "The Effect of Business Conditions on Early Judicial Decisions Concerning Restraint of Trade." *J Econ Hist,* X (1950), 30-44.

7 CHANDLER, Alfred D., Jr. "The Organization of Manufacturing and Transportation." See **57.**5, 137-151, with comments, 152-165.

8 CHANDLER, Alfred D., Jr. *Strategy and Structure: Chapters in the History of the Industrial Enterprise.* Cambridge, Mass., 1862.†

9 COCHRAN, Thomas C. *Railroad Leaders, 1845-1890: The Business Mind in Action.* Cambridge, Mass., 1953.

10 DODD, Edwin M. *American Business Corporations until 1860: with Special Reference to Massachusetts.* Cambridge, Mass., 1954.

11 NEU, Irene D. *Erastus Corning: Merchant and Financier, 1794-1872.* Ithaca, 1960.

12 RESSEGUIE, Harry E. "Alexander Turney Stewart and the Development of the Department Store, 1823-1876." *Bus Hist Rev,* XXXIX (1965), 301-322.

13 ROEDER, Robert E. "Merchants of Ante-Bellum New Orleans." *Explo Entrep Hist,* X (1958), 113-122.

14 SCHEIBER, Harry N. "Entrepreneurship and Western Development, the Case of Micajah T. Williams." *Bus Hist Rev,* XXXVII (1963), 345-368.

15 THROCKMORTON, Arthur L. "The Role of the Merchant on the Oregon Frontier: The Early Business Career of Henry W. Corbett, 1851-1869." *J Econ Hist,* XVI (1956), 539-550.

16 WOHL, R. R. *Henry Noble Day: A Study in Good Works, 1880-1890.* See **8.**23.

17 WOODMAN, Harold D. "Itinerant Cotton Merchants of the Ante-Bellum South." *Ag Hist,* XL (1966), 79-90.

18 WYATT-BROWN, Bertram. "God and Dun & Bradstreet, 1841-1851." *Bus Hist Rev,* XL (1966), 432-450.

18. Government and Business

1 BENSON, Lee. *Merchants, Farmers & Railroads: Railroad Regulation and New York Politics, 1850-1887.* Cambridge, Mass., 1955.

2 BROUDE, Henry W. "The Role of the State in American Economic Development, 1820-1890." *The State and Economic Growth.* Ed. Hugh G. J. Aitken. New York, 1959, 4-25.

3 EISELEN, Malcolm R. *Rise of Pennsylvania Protectionism.* Philadelphia, 1932.

4 Federal Coordinator of Transportation. *Public Aids to Transportation.* 4 vols. Washington, D.C., 1938-1940.

5 FINE, Sidney. *Laissez Faire and the General-Welfare State: A Study of Conflict in American Thought, 1865-1901.* Ann Arbor, 1956.†

6 GOODRICH, Carter and Harvey H. SEGAL. "Baltimore's Aid to Railroads: A Study in the Municipal Planning of Internal Improvements." *J Econ Hist,* XIII (1953), 2-35.

7 GOODRICH, Carter. *Government Promotion of American Canals and Railroads.* New York, 1960.

8 HARTZ, Louis. "Government-Business Relations," with comment. See 57.5, 83-116.

9 HOFSTADTER, Richard. "The Tariff Issue on the Eve of the Civil War." *Am Hist Rev,* XLIV (1938), 50-55.

10 LIVELY, Robert A. "The American System: A Review Article." *Bus Hist Rev,* XXIX (1955), 81-96. (A critical appraisal of the leading writings on the role of government in economic life.)

11 MC KEE, Marguerite M. *The Ship Subsidy Question in United States Politics. Stud Hist* (Smith). Northampton, Mass., 1922.

12 MARTIN, Thomas P. "Free Trade and the Oregon Question, 1842-1846." See 8.11, 470-491.

13 MEEKER, Royal. *History of Shipping Subsidies.* New York, 1905.

14 NASH, Gerald D. *State Government and Economic Development: A History of Administrative Policies in California, 1849-1933.* Berkeley, 1964.

15 PRIMM, James N. *Economic Policy in the Development of a Western State, Missouri, 1820-1860.* Cambridge, Mass., 1954.

16 REMINI, Robert V. "Martin Van Buren and the Tariff of Abominations." *Am Hist Rev,* LXIII (1958), 903-917.

17 TAYLOR, George Rogers, ed. *The Great Tariff Debate, 1820-1830.* Boston, 1953.†

NOTES

INDEX

A–B

Abernethy, T. P., **31**.12
Abramovitz, Moses, **2**.7, 8, **7**.22
Adams, Donald R., Jr., **47**.11
Adams, Henry C., **15**.19, **33**.8, **48**.5, **48**.6
Adams, J. T., **16**.19, **18**.1, **18**.2, **35**.15.
Adams, Nathaniel, **59**.5
Adams, Ramon F., **11**.3
Adams, T. M., **51**.2
Adams, William F., **61**.1
Adler, Dorothy R., **71**.8
Aitken, Hugh G. J., **2**.9, **8**.1, **49**.13
Albion, Robert G., **11**.4, **36**.13, **42**.1, **59**.7, **69**.5
Alexander, E. P., **71**.9
Allen, Harry C., **63**.9
Allen, Turner W., **40**.8
Ambler, Charles H., **13**.1
Anderson, C. Arnold, **8**.2
Andreano, Ralph L., **6**.11
Andrews, Charles M., **24**.19, **30**.4, **31**.13
Andrews, Israel D., **56**.1
Angas, W. Mack, **69**.6
Appleton, Nathan, **44**.18
Arena, C. Richard, **42**.2
Arky, Louis, **80**.7
Armroyd, George, **67**.8
Arndt, Karl J. R., **38**.1
Arrington, Leonard J., **58**.11, **77**.2, **87**.2
Ashley, M. P., **30**.5
Ashley, W. J., **2**.10
Ashton, T. S., **2**.11
Athearn, Robert G., **65**.2
Atherton, L. E., **42**.3, **87**.3, **87**.4, **87**.5

Babson, David L., **24**.13
Bagnall, William R., **26**.19
Bahret, James L., **37**.9
Bailyn, Bernard, **23**.5, **25**.1, **25**.2, **79**.2
Bailyn, Lotte, **25**.2
Baker, G. P., **71**.10
Baldwin, Joseph G., **85**.6
Baldwin, Leland D., **40**.9, **45**.4
Balinky, Alexander S., **48**.7
Ballagh, James C., **8**.3, **20**.18, **27**.14
Bamford, Paul W., **42**.4
Bancroft, Frederic, **81**.17
Baran, Paul, **4**.7

Barber, William D., **48**.8
Bardhan, Pranab, **2**.12
Barker, C. A., **31**.14
Barker, T. C., **25**.3
Barnes, Viola F., **20**.19
Barnett, Harold J., **66**.8
Barnhart, John D., **38**.2
Barraclough, Geoffrey, **63**.10
Barrow, Thomas C., **30**.6
Barton, Glen T., **62**.19
Bassett, John S., **31**.15
Bassett, T. D. Seymour, **59**.8, **59**.9
Batchelder, Samuel, **44**.19
Bates, William W., **13**.2
Bathe, Dorothy, **45**.5, **45**.6
Bathe, Greville, **45**.5, **45**.6
Battison, Edwin A., **45**.7
Baudet, H., **4**.8
Baughman, James P., **67**.14, **71**.11
Baxter, W. T., **23**.6
Bayley, Rafael A., **48**.9
Beach, M. Y., **57**.15
Beame, Edmond M., **77**.3
Beard, Charles A., **54**.6, **55**.4
Beard, Mary, **9**.15
Beaton, Kendall, **66**.2
Beer, George L., **30**.7, **30**.8, **30**.9
Belcher, W. W., **59**.10
Bell, Herbert C., **25**.4
Belz, Herman J., **28**.12
Bemis, S. F., **42**.5, **42**.6
Benedict, C. Harry, **66**.3
Bennett, M. K., **20**.20
Bennett, Norman R., **42**.7
Benns, Frank Lee, **42**.8
Benson, George C. S., **15**.20
Benson, Lee, **88**.1
Benton, Elbert J., **73**.18
Bernstein, Leonard, **80**.8
Berrill, K., **13**.3
Berry, Thomas, **51**.3, **87**.6
Berthoff, Rowland T., **37**.10
Bestor, Arthur E., Jr., **9**.16
Bezanson, Anne, **28**.13, **51**.4, **51**.5, **79**.3
Bidwell, Percy W., **11**.5, **38**.3, **38**.4
Bigelow, Bruce M., **23**.7
Billias, George A., **28**.14
Billington, Ray A., **11**.6, **11**.7, **16**.20, **63**.11, **63**.12, **63**.13, **63**.14
Bimba, Anthony, **9**.17
Binder, Frederick M., **77**.4
Bining, Arthur C., **6**.12, **26**.20, **30**.10, **45**.8

INDEX   B–C

Bishop, Avard L., **69.**7
Bishop, J. L., **14.**14
Bjork, Gordon C., **34.**3, **42.**9, **51.**6
Blake, N. M., **36.**14
Blandi, Joseph G., **52.**1
Blicksilver, Jack, **77.**5
Blodget, Samuel, **33.**10
Bode, Carl, **56.**14
Bogart, Ernest L., **48.**10, **67.**15, **73.**19
Bogen, Jules I., **71.**12
Bogle, Victor M., **59.**11, **59.**12, **59.**13
Bogue, Allan G., **61.**17, **63.**15
Bogue, Margaret B., **61.**18, **63.**15
Bolino, August C., **6.**13
Bolles, Albert S., **14.**15, **48.**11
Bolton, Ethel S., **19.**20
Boman, Martha, **59.**14
Bond, Beverley W., **21.**1
Bonner, James C., **11.**8
Boorstin, Daniel J., **77.**6
Bourne, Edward G., **82.**20
Bowden, William H., **25.**5
Bowen, Eli, **65.**20
Bowen, Frank C., **69.**8
Bower, Robert T., **80.**9
Bowman, Albert H., **55.**5
Bowman, Mary Jean, **8.**2
Boyd, Thomas A., **45.**9
Bradlee, Francis B. C., **42.**10
Brady, Dorothy S., **51.**7, **51.**8
Bramson, Roy T., **75.**14
Branch, E. Douglas, **66.**4
Brebner, John Bartlet, **8.**4
Bremner, Robert H., **8.**5, **80.**10
Brewer, Thomas B., **6.**18, **45.**10
Brewster, William, **18.**3, **20.**1
Bridenbaugh, Carl, **17.**1, **17.**2, **18.**4, **27.**1
Bridenbaugh, Jessica, **18.**4
Brigham, Clarence S., **1.**4
Brissot, J. P., **24.**14
Brogan, D. W., **54.**7
Bronson, Henry, **28.**15
Brooks, George E., Jr., **42.**7
Brooks, Robert P., **15.**21
Broshar, Helen, **23.**8
Broude, Henry W., **2.**13, **88.**2
Brown, A. Theodore, **8.**13
Brown, B. Katherine, **31.**17
Brown, Cecil K., **71.**13
Brown, John C., **49.**14
Brown, K. L., **83.**14
Brown, Richard M., **18.**5

Brown, Robert E., **31.**16, **31.**17, **31.**19, **54.**8
Bruce, Kathleen, **11.**9, **61.**19
Bruce, P. A., **18.**6
Bruce, Robert V., **56.**17
Bruchey, Stuart, **5.**1, **5.**3, **6.**14, **6.**16, **11.**10, **23.**9, **42.**11, **48.**12, **50.**11
Buck, E. H., **20.**2
Buck, Norman S., **42.**12
Buck, Solon J., **20.**2, **38.**5, **38.**6
Budd, Edward C., **56.**15
Buel, Richard, Jr., **31.**18
Bullock, Charles J., **28.**16, **48.**13, **73.**20
Burgess, George H., **71.**14
Burlingame, Roger, **75.**15
Buron, Edmond, **42.**13
Burnstein, M. L., **28.**17
Burt, A. L., **42.**14

Cadman, John W., Jr., **52.**2
Caine, M. B., **16.**10
Caldwell, Stephen A., **49.**15
Calhoun, Daniel H., **45.**11
Callender, Guy Stevens, **6.**15, **52.**3
Calvert, Monte A., **56.**16, **80.**11
Carey, Lewis J., **17.**3
Carey, Mathew, **69.**3
Carlton, Frank T., **79.**4
Carman, Harry J., **71.**15, **75.**16
Carosso, Vincent P., **7.**18
Carothers, Neil, **49.**16
Carpenter, Clifford E., **61.**20
Carrier, Lyman, **21.**2
Carson, Jane, **18.**7
Carstensen, Vernon, **63.**16
Carter, E. C., II, **49.**17
Caruso, John A., **20.**3
Cary, John, **31.**19
Cathey, Cornelius O., **38.**7
Catlin, George B., **22.**11
Catterall, Ralph C., **83.**15
Caughey, John W., **64.**15
Cave, Alfred A., **1.**5
Chadbourne, W. W., **49.**18
Chaddock, Robert E., **49.**19
Chambers, E. J., **5.**2
Champagne, Roger J., **31.**20, **31.**21, **32.**1
Chandler, Alfred D., Jr., **5.**3, **6.**16, **71.**16, **71.**17, **86.**1, **87.**7, **87.**8
Chandler, Charles L., **42.**15, **42.**16
Chapelle, Howard I., **69.**9, **69.**10

INDEX

C–D

Chapman, Leonard B., 27.2
Chase, Henry, 56.2
Chevalier, Michael, 56.3
Cheyney, Edward P., 63.17
Chickering, Jesse, 9.14, 60.18
Chittenden, Hiram M., 38.8
Chiu, Ping, 79.5
Christman, Henry, 58.12
Cist, Charles, 59.6
Clapham, Sir John, 2.14
Clark, A. H., 2.15, 69.11
Clark, Colin, 2.16
Clark, Dora Mae, 27.15
Clark, John G., 74.1, 74.2
Clark, Malcolm C., 77.7
Clark, Thomas D., 1.6, 11.11, 74.3
Clark, Victor S., 14.16
Clark, W. H., 67.16
Clauder, Anna C., 42.17
Clawson, Marion, 11.12
Clemen, Alexander, 11.13
Clemen, R. A., 45.12
Cleveland, Frederick A., 71.18
Clough, Shepard B., 6.17, 86.2
Clowse, Converse D., 25.6
Coatsworth, John H., 42.18
Cochran, Thomas C., 2.17, 2.18, 6.12, 6.18, 8.6, 77.8, 87.9
Coffin, Margaret, 45.13
Cole, Arthur H., 3.1, 3.2, 8.7, 14.17, 16.1, 23.10, 28.18, 33.11, 51.15, 62.1, 63.18, 77.9, 86.3
Cole, Donald B., 59.15
Cole, W. A., 25.7
Coleman, Kenneth, 32.2
Coleman, Peter J., 28.19, 58.13
Colles, Christopher, 40.6
Collier, Christopher, 48.14
Colman, Gould P., 62.2
Colwell, Stephen, 83.8
Cometti, Elizabeth, 51.9
Commons, John R., 7.1, 9.18, 47.10, 79.6, 79.7
Conrad, Alfred H., 5.3, 5.14, 5.19, 9.19, 10.1
Cooke, Jacob E., 33.18, 55.6
Cooney, E. W., 86.4
Cootner, Paul H., 71.19
Copeland, Melvin T., 45.14
Cotterill, R. S., 38.9, 38.10, 71.20, 71.21, 74.4
Cowl, Philip A., 53.8
Coxe, Tench, 33.12, 41.16, 45.1
Coyne, F. E., 14.18

Craib, Roderick H., 13.4
Craig, Neville B., 36.8
Crampton, Charles G., 66.5
Crandall, Ruth, 2.3, 28.20
Crane, Verner W., 18.8
Cranmer, H. Jerome, 69.12, 69.16
Craven, Avery O., 21.3
Craven, W. F., 18.9
Crawford, Walter F., 25.8
Crittenden, C. C., 22.12, 25.9
Crocker, George G., 67.17
Crosby, Alfred W., Jr., 42.19
Cummings, Hubertis M., 40.10
Curti, Merle E., 63.19
Cutler, Carl C., 40.11, 69.13

Dain, Floyd R., 35.16
Dangerfield, George, 34.6
Danhof, Clarence H., 39.18, 62.3, 63.20, 63.21
Daniells, Lorna M., 1.7
Daniels, G. W., 42.20
Darling, Arthur B., 80.12
David, Paul A., 34.7, 62.4, 75.3
Davidson, Philip, 32.3
Davidson, Sol, 64.10
Davies, K. G., 23.11
Davis, Andrew M., 28.9, 29.1
Davis, David Brion, 10.2
Davis, Joseph S., 52.4
Davis, Lance E., 5.5, 5.6, 5.7, 7.2, 49.21, 77.10, 77.11, 82.21, 84.13, 86.5, 86.6, 86.7
Davis, William T., 18.10
Davison, Robert A., 23.12
Davisson, William I., 18.11, 29.2
Day, Clarence A., 11.14
Day, Clive, 75.17
Dearing, Charles L., 67.18
De Bow, J. D. B., 35.12, 56.4
De Camp, L. Sprague, 45.15
Decker, Leslie E., 82.22
Defebaugh, James E., 11.15
Demaree, A. L., 11.16
Denison, Edward F., 56.15
Dennett, Tyler, 42.21
Depew, C. M., 34.8
Derrick, Samuel M., 71.22
Derry, T. K., 14.19
Desai, Meghnad, Jr., 5.8
De Voto, Bernard, 64.1
Dew, Charles B., 77.12

INDEX

D–F

Dewey, Davis R., **16.**2, **50.**1 **50.**9, 83.16
Deyrup, Felicia J., **45.**16
Diamond, Sigmund, **17.**4
Dick, Everett, **64.**2
Dickerson, O. M. **30.**11, **32.**4
Dill, Augustus G., **47.**12
Dillard, Dudley, **8.**8
Dillistin, W. H., **83.**17
Dixon, F. H., **43.**1
Dodd, Edwin M., **87.**10
Dodd, Merrick E., **52.**5
Dolan, J. R., **13.**5
Donahue, Gilbert E., **10.**18
Donnan, Elizabeth, **24.**15, **25.**10
Donnell, E. J., **62.**5
Dorfman, Joseph, **8.**9, **17.**5, **34.**9, **80.**13
Dorsey, Dorothy B., **51.**10
Dorsey, Rhoda M., **43.**2
Douds, Howard C., **23.**13
Douglass, Elisha P., **32.**5
Douglass, William, **28.**10
Dow, George F., **25.**11
Dowd, Douglas F., **64.**3
Drake, Daniel, **36.**9
Drake, Milton, **1.**8
Drummond, Ian M., **79.**8
Dubester, Henry J., **37.**11
Du Bois, W. E. B. **10.**3, **47.**12
Dudley, J. G., **76.**20
Dulles, Foster Rhea, **10.**4
Dunaway, Wayland F., **20.**4, **69.**14
Dunn, Edgar S., Jr., **9.**2
Dunne, Gerald T., **83.**18
Dupree, A. Hunter, **56.**17
Durant, Captain Edward W., **66.**6
Durrenberger, J. A., **40.**12
Dutton, William S., **75.**18
Dwight, Timothy, **35.**13, **36.**10
Dyer, Walter A., **27.**16, **54.**9

East, Robert A., **23.**14, **53.**9, **53.**10
Easterlin, Richard A., **3.**3, **57.**3, **58.**14
Eaton, Clement, **8.**10
Eavenson, Howard N., **66.**7
Edelman, Edward, **23.**15
Edward, A. Wyatt, IV, **59.**16
Edwards, Everett E., **1.**9, **1.**10
Eiselen, Malcolm R., **88.**3
Elazar, Daniel J., **52.**6
Eliasberg, Vera F., **66.**8

Elkins, Stanley, **54.**10, **57.**4, **81.**18
Ellertsen, E. Peter, **29.**3
Elliott, Orrin L., **52.**7
Ellis, David M., **38.**11, **74.**5
Ellsworth, Lucius, **38.**12
Ely, Roland T., **74.**6
Engelman, F. L., **32.**6
Engerman, Stanley L., **81.**19
Ernst, Joseph A., **29.**4
Ernst, Robert, **61.**2
Esarey, Logan, **50.**2, **67.**19
Evans Charles H., **13.**6
Evans, Emory G., **23.**16
Evans, G. H., Jr., **52.**8, **86.**8
Evans, Oliver, **45.**2
Eversley, D. E. C., **10.**7
Ewing, John S., **77.**13
Ezell, John, **16.**3, **29.**5

Fabricant, S., **3.**4
Fairchild, Bryon, **23.**17
Falconer, John I., **11.**5
Farnam, H. W., **79.**9
Faulkner, Harold U., **7.**3
Fee, Walter R., **35.**17
Feer, Robert A., **18.**12
Feldman, Egal, **27.**3
Felt, Joseph B., **28.**11
Fenichel, Ross M., **75.**19
Fenstermaker, J. Van, **50.**3, **50.**4
Ferguson, E. James, **29.**6, **48.**15, **53.**11
Ferguson, Eugene S., **1.**11
Fields, Emmett B., **62.**6
Fine, Sidney, **88.**5
Fingerhut, Eugene R., **53.**12
Fischbaum, Marvin, **81.**20
Fisher, Marvin, **76.**1
Fishlow, Albert, **4.**9, **34.**3, **57.**1, **69.**15, **72.**1, **72.**2, **74.**7, **79.**10
Fiske, John, **54.**11
Fitch, James M., **77.**14
Fite, Gilbert C., **7.**4
Fletcher, S. W., **11.**17
Flexner, James T., **40.**13
Flick, Alexander C., **19.**3
Fogel R. W., **5.**3, **5.**9, **5.**10, **5.**11, **5.**12, **72.**3
Folsom, William H. C., **66.**9
Foner, Philip S., **10.**5, **82.**1
Forbes, Allan W., **27.**17
Forrest, William S., **36.**11
Foulds, Margaret H., **50.**5

INDEX

Fox, Dixon R., 35.18
Fox, William F., 11.18
Francis, W. H., 45.3
Franklin, John H., 47.13
Frantz, Joe B., 64.15
Frederick, James V., 68.1
Freedley, Edwin T., 75.9
French, Allen, 20.5
Frickey, Edwin, 86.3
Fuller, Grace P., 45.17

Gagliardo, John G., 21.4
Galambos, Louis, 3.5, 6.16
Gallatin, Albert, 41.17, 48.5, 83.9, 83.10
Gallman, Robert E., 57.1, 57.2, 62.7
Galpin, William F., 43.3, 43.4
Gara, Larry, 64.4
Garber, John P., 8.12
Gares, Albert J., 43.5
Gatell, Frank O., 83.19, 83.20, 84.1, 85.7
Gates, Paul W., 11.19, 38.13, 62.8, 62.9, 62.10, 64.5, 64.6, 64.7, 64.8, 72.4, 72.5
Gates, William B., 66.10
Geiser, K. F., 27.18
Genovese, Eugene D., 10.6, 57.4, 62.11, 82.2, 82.3
Gephart, William F., 35.19
Gerhard, Dietrich, 64.9
Gerschenkron, Alexander, 3.6
Gerstner, Franz A., 67.9
Gibb, George S., 45.18, 77.15
Gibson, George H., 47.14, 77.16, 77.17
Giddens, Paul H., 25.13
Giesecke, Albert A., 30.12
Gilchrist, David T., 36.15, 57.5
Gillespie, W. M., 67.10
Gillingham, Harold E., 25.14
Gilmore, Eugene A., 47.10
Ginger, Ray, 79.11
Gipson, Lawrence H., 17.7, 21.5, 29.7, 32.7, 32.8
Glaab, Charles N., 7.5, 8.13, 72.6
Glade, William P., 3.7
Glass, D. V., 10.7
Glen, Bess, 68.10
Glover, Frederick J., 74.8
Goebel, Dorothy B., 25.15
Gold, August B., 76.2
Goldman, Eric F., 36.19

Goldman, Henry H., 74.9
Goldsmith, Raymond W., 8.14, 34.11
Goldstein, Sidney, 61.6
Golembe, Carter H., 84.2
Goode, George B., 11.20
Goodman, Paul, 17.8, 45.19, 54.12
Goodman, Warren H., 55.7
Goodrich, Carter, 1.12, 5.13, 52.9, 52.10, 61.3, 64.10, 69.16, 88.6, 88.7
Gordon, D. F. 5.2
Gottlieb, Manuel, 76.3, 76.4
Gouge, William M., 83.11, 83.12
Gould, Clarence P., 18.13, 22.13, 29.8
Gould, E. W., 69.17
Govan, Thomas P., 84.3
Graham, G. S., 69.18
Graham, Ian C. C., 20.6
Grampp, William D., 55.8
Grant, Charles S., 18.14
Grant, E. B., 71.6
Gras, N. S. B., 4.10, 4.11, 35.5, 50.6
Gray, Lewis C., 11.21
Gray, Ralph D., 40.14, 45.20
Gray, Robert D., 51.5
Greef, Albert O., 86.9
Greeley, Horace, 75.10
Green, Constance McLaughlin, 36.16, 36.17, 45.21, 59.17, 59.18
Greene, E. B., 17.9, 20.7
Greene, Jack P., 29.9
Greenhut, Melvin L., 8.15
Greer, Thomas H., 51.11
Greever, William S., 66.11
Gregg, Dorothy, 46.1
Gregg, Josiah, 74.10
Gregg, William, 75.11
Griffin, Clifford S., 34.12
Griffin, Richard W., 46.2, 47.3, 76.5, 77.18, 77.19, 77.20, 77.21, 78.20, 80.14
Griswold, A. Whitney, 18.15
Gurley, John G., 52.21

Habakkuk, H. J., 46.3, 76.6, 85.8
Hacker, Louis M., 5.14, 7.6, 32.9, 34.13
Hall, Courtney R., 46.4
Hall, James, 57.16, 57.17, 57.18, 57.19
Haller, William, 30.13
Hamilton, Alexander, 33.13

INDEX

H

Hammond, Bray, **16**.4, **84**.4, **84**.5
Hammond, M. B., **12**.1
Hammond, Seth, **46**.5
Hancock, Harold B., **46**.6
Handlin, Mary, **27**.19, **52**.12
Handlin, Oscar, **10**.8, **27**.19, **37**.12, **52**.11, **52**.12
Hanna, Mary A., **25**.16
Hannay, Agnes, **46**.7
Hansen, M. L., **10**.9
Hanson, K. R., **78**.1
Hardin, Thomas L., **68**.2
Harley, R. Bruce, **21**.6
Harlow, Alvin F., **40**.15, **68**.3, **72**.7, **72**.8
Harlow, Ralph V., **35**.20
Harper, Lawrence A., **1**.13, **30**.14, **30**.15, **32**.10
Harriman, D. G., **13**.7
Harrington, V. D., **20**.7, **23**.18
Harris, Marshall, **21**.7
Harris, Seymour E., **7**.7
Harroun, Catherine, **75**.1
Harte, C. R., **78**.5
Hartley, E. N., **21**.19
Hartsough, M. L., **40**.16
Hartwell, R. M., **3**.8
Hartz, Louis, **52**.13, **79**.12, **88**.8
Hasse, A. R., **1**.14
Hatcher, Harlan, **40**.17, **40**.18
Havighurst, Walter, **20**.8
Hawgood, John A., **64**.11
Hawk, Emory Q., **8**.16
Hawk, G. R., **5**.16
Hayward, John, **56**.6
Haywood, C. Robert, **21**.8, **27**.20
Hazard, Blanche E., **15**.1
Hazel, Joseph A., **62**.12
Heath, Milton, **52**.14, **72**.9
Heaton, Herbert, **37**.13
Hedges, James B., **23**.19
Hedges, Joseph E., **84**.6
Hedrick, Ulysses P., **12**.2, **12**.3
Helderman, Leonard C., **50**.7
Helper, Hinton R., **57**.20
Hemphill, John, II, **25**.17, **30**.16
Henderson, Elizabeth K., **38**.14
Henlein, Paul C., **38**.15, **62**.13
Henretta, James A., **18**.16
Henry, Robert S., **72**.10
Hepburn, A. B., **50**.8
Herfindahl, Orris C., **66**.12
Herndon, G. M., **46**.8
Herrick, Cheesman A., **10**.10

Heston, Alan, **74**.15
Heubner, Solomon, **86**.10
Hibbard, B. H., **38**.16
Hickcox, John H., **29**.10
Hidy, Muriel, **72**.11
Hidy, Ralph W., **16**.5, **72**.11, **84**.7
Hill, Forest G., **40**.19
Hilliard, Samuel B., **74**.11
Hindle, Brooke, **15**.2
Hinshaw, Clifford R., Jr., **69**.19
Hirschman, Albert O., **3**.9
Hoagland, H. E., **40**.20
Hobsbawm, Ernest, **4**.7
Hodge, Charles L., **72**.12
Hofstadter, Richard, **80**.15, **88**.9
Hogan, William R., **8**.17, **64**.12
Hohman, Elmo P. **12**.4, **27**.21
Holdsworth, John T., **16**.6, **50**.9
Hollander, J. H., **16**.7
Holmes, Oliver W., **40**.21
Holmes, William F., **41**.1, **68**.4
Homans, Isaac Smith, **13**.8, **13**.9
Homans, J. Smith, **13**.8
Homans, J. Smith, Jr., **13**.8, **13**.9
Homer, Sidney, **86**.11
Hoogenboom, Ari A., **17**.15, **25**.18
Hooker, Roland M., **25**.19
Hoover, Edgar M., **3**.10
Hoover, Ethel D., **16**.15, **85**.9
Hopkins, James F., **38**.17
Hornung, C. P., **13**.10
Horsman, Reginald, **55**.9
House, Albert V., **61**.14
Hubach, Robert R., **1**.15
Hughes, H. Stuart, **3**.11
Hughes, J. R. T., **5**.7, **5**.15, **7**.2, **8**.18, **49**.21, **85**.10
Hughson, Shirley C., **25**.20
Hugins, Walter, **80**.16
Hulbert, Archer B., **13**.11, **13**.12
Hungerford, Edward, **72**.13, **72**.14
Hunt, E. H., **5**.16, **5**.17
Hunt, Freeman, **87**.1
Hunter, Dard, **27**.4
Hunter, Louis C., **35**.21, **69**.20, **78**.2, **78**.3, **78**.4
Hunter, Robert F., **41**.2, **68**.5
Hunter, William C., **54**.13
Huntington, C. C., **50**.10, **70**.3
Hurst, James Willard, **64**.13, **66**.13
Huse, C. P., **59**.19
Hussey, M., **51**.5
Hutcheson, Harold, **34**.14
Hutchins, John G. B., **1**.16, **46**.9

100

INDEX

H–L

Hutchinson, A. E., **85**.11
Hutchinson, William T., **76**.7

Imlah, Albert H., **43**.6
Ingalls, W. R., **38**.18, **66**.14
Innis, Harold A., **12**.5, **22**.1
Isard, Walter, **3**.12, **4**.12, **46**.10
Ise, John, **64**.14

Jackson, Clayton, **68**.6
Jackson, G. Gibbard, **69**.21
Jackson, Harry F., **41**.3
Jackson, Sidney L., **80**.17
Jackson, W. Turrentine, **68**.7
Jacobs, Wilbur R., **22**.2, **64**.15
James, F. Cyril, **84**.8
James, Marquis, **86**.12
Jameson, John F., **25**.21, **53**.13
Jellison, Richard M., **29**.9, **29**.11
Jenks, Leland H., **72**.15, **86**.13
Jennings, Sister Marietta, **43**.7
Jennings, Walter W., **55**.10
Jensen, Arthur L., **26**.1, **30**.17
Jensen, Merrill, **32**.11, **38**.19, **54**.14
Jernegan, Marcus W., **27**.22
Jewett, Fred E., **48**.16
Johnson, Arthur M., **72**.16
Johnson, E. A. J., **17**.10
Johnson, Emory R., **13**.13
Johnson, Keach, **27**.5
Johnson, R. C., **29**.12
Johnson, Victor L., **23**.20, **53**.14
Jones, Chester L., **69**.22
Jones, Fred M., **43**.8
Jones, Herbert G., **22**.14
Jones, Maldwyn A., **10**.11
Jones, Newton B., **30**.18
Jones, Peter d'a, **7**.8
Jordan, Philip D., **41**.4
Jordan, Terry G., **61**.4
Jordan, Weymouth T., **59**.20, **62**.14
Jordan, Winthrop D., **27**.23
Jorgensen, Charles J., **68**.8
Josephson, Hannah, **80**.18
Judah, Charles B., Jr., **22**.3

Kaiser, Carl W., Jr., **52**.15
Karn, Edwin D., **9**.4
Keiler, Hans, **70**.1
Keith, H. C., **78**.5
Kemmerer, Donald L., **29**.13, **62**.15

Kendrick, John W., **85**.9
Kennedy, Charles J., **72**.17, **72**.18, **73**.16
Kennedy, Miles C., **71**.14
Kenyon, Cecilia M., **34**.15
Kessler, W. C., **52**.16, **52**.17
Kettell, Thomas P., **58**.1
Kimball, Gertrude S., **43**.9
Kimmel, Lewis H., **48**.17
Kincaid, Robert L., **22**.15
Kindleberger, C. P., **43**.10
Kingsbury, Susan M., **81**.6
Kingsford, William, **67**.11
Kinley, David, **82**.23, **83**.1
Kirkland, Edward C., **7**.9, **68**.9
Kistler, Thelma M., **72**.19
Klebaner, Benjamin J., **80**.19
Klein, Herbert S., **10**.12
Klein, Judith L. V., **62**.19
Klein, Milton M., **32**.12
Klimm, Lester E., **37**.14
Klingaman, David, **43**.11
Klose, Nelson, **12**.6
Knollenberg, Bernhard, **32**.13
Knowlton, Evelyn H., **78**.6
Kohlmeier, Albert L., **30**.19, **74**.12
Kohn, David, **68**.10
Kranzberg, Melvin, **15**.3
Krenkel, John H., **68**.11
Kroeber, Clifton B., **65**.18
Krooss, Herman E., **7**.10, **16**.13, **50**.11
Kuczynski, Jürgen, **10**.13
Kuhlmann, Charles B., **15**.4
Kuznets, Simon, **3**.13, **4**.13, **8**.19, **8**.20, **34**.11, **34**.16

Labaree, Benjamin, **18**.17, **24**.1
Labaree, Leonard W., **17**.11
La Force, J. C., **84**.9
Laing, J., **38**.20
Lake, Wilfred S., **50**.12
Lalli, Michael, **37**.15
Lamar, Howard R., **58**.15
Lamb, Robert K., **34**.17, **60**.1
Lambert, John, **33**.14
Lammons, Frank B., **68**.12
Lampard, Eric E., **8**.21, **9**.2, **62**.16
Land, Aubrey C., **18**.18, **18**.19
Lander, Ernest M., Jr., **46**.11, **46**.12, **47**.15
Landes, David, **17**.12, **46**.13
Lane, Carl D., **70**.2

INDEX L–M

Lane, Frederic C., 7.11
Lane, Wheaton J., 13.14, 41.5, 41.6
Lanier, Mary J., 26.2
La Rouchefoucauld-Liancourt, F. A., 33.15
Larson, Agnes M., 66.15
Larson, Henrietta M., 1.17
Lathrop, W. G., 46.14
Latimer, Margaret K., 55.11
Lawson, M. G., 22.4
Layer, Robert G., 81.1
Leach, Douglas E., 20.9
Leavitt, Charles T., 38.21
Lebergott, Stanley, 47.16, 47.17, 47.18, 68.13
Le Duc, Thomas, 39.1, 64.16, 64.17
Lee, Anne S., 61.5
Lee, Everett, 37.15, 61.5
Legler, John, 82.21
Leiman, Melvin M., 58.16
Lemon, James T., 19.1, 21.9
Lent, D. Geneva, 64.18
Lester, Richard A., 29.14
Lewis, Archibald R., 64.19
Lewis, George E., 39.2
Lewis, W. David, 57.5
Leyland, H. T., 46.15
Libby, O. G., 54.15
Lincoln, Charles H., 32.14
Lincoln, Jonathan T., 46.16
Linden, Fabian, 76.8, 82.4
Lippincott, Horace M., 19.2
Lippincott, Isaac, 13.15, 76.9
Littlefield, Henry M., 64.20
Litwack, Leon F., 79.13
Lively, Robert A., 88.10
Livermore, Shaw, 39.3, 52.18
Livingood, James W., 43.12
Lockridge, Kenneth A., 20.10
Lokken, Roscoe, L., 64.21
Lord, Eleanor L., 27.6
Losse, Winifred J., 43.13
Love, W. De Loss, 13.16
Lovejoy, David S., 32.15
Lovett, Robert W., 43.14, 46.17
Lower, R. M., 64.22
Ludlum, D. M., 35.22
Lydon, James G., 26.3, 26.4
Lynd, Staughton, 32.16
Lynn, Robert A., 86.14
Lyon, Peter, 78.7

Mabry, W. A., 43.15

McAnear, Beverly, 28.1
McBee, Alice E., 79.14
McClelland, C. P., 70.3
McClelland, David C., 3.14
McClelland, Peter D., 5.18, 72.20
McColley, Robert, 47.19
McCorison, Marcus A., 46.18
McCrum, Blanche P., 1.18
McCulloch, J. R., 56.9
McCusker, John J., 22.16
MacDonald, Allan, 60.2
McDonald, Forrest, 53.15, 54.16
McDougall, D. M., 7.2
Macesich, George, 74.13, 84.10, 84.11
McFarland, Raymond, 12.7
McGann, Paul W., 66.8, 66.12
McGann, Thomas F., 64.19
MacGill, Caroline E., 13.17
McGouldrick, Paul F., 46.19, 77.10
McGrane, Reginald C., 83.2, 85.12
McKay, Richard C., 13.18
McKee, Marguerite M., 88.11
McKee, Samuel, Jr., 19.3, 28.2
McKelvey, Blake, 36.18
McKitrick, Eric, 54.10
McKitrick, Reuben, 65.1
McLendon, James H., 39.4
McMaster, John B., 43.16
McMaster, Richard K., 24.16
McNair, J. B., 78.8
McNall, Neil A., 39.5
Macpherson, David, 16.18
Maginnis, Arthur J., 70.4
Mailloux, Kenneth, 46.20
Main, Jackson T., 36.1, 39.6, 53.16, 53.17, 54.17, 54.18
Makinson, David H., 26.5
Malone, Joseph J., 22.5
Malone, M. S., 24.2
Manning, William, 55.3
Marburg, Theodore, 6.17, 43.17, 78.9
Mark, Irving, 21.10
Marlowe, George F., 41.7
Marti, Donald B., 39.7
Martin, Alfred S., 30.20
Martin, Edgar W., 81.2
Martin, J. G., 50.13
Martin, Margaret E., 24.3
Martin, Robert F., 34.18
Martin, Thomas P., 88.12
Martin, William E., 68.14
Marx, Leo, 8.22

INDEX

M–O

Mason, B., **53**.18
Masters, Donald C., **74**.14
Matthews, R. C. O., **85**.13
Mayer, Kurt B., **36**.2, **61**.6
Mayo, Bernard, **36**.19
Mease, James, **36**.13
Meeker, Royal, **88**.13
Meier, Gerald M., **3**.15
Mendenhall, Marjorie S., **39**.8
Menn, J. K., **82**.5
Meriwether, Robert L., **19**.4
Merrens, H. R., **19**.5
Merton, Robert K., **76**.10
Mesick, Jane L., **13**.19
Meyer, Duane, **20**.11
Meyer, John R., **5**.4, **5**.19, **10**.1, **58**.17
Middleton, Arthur P., **26**.6
Miles Pliny, **73**.17
Miller, Douglas T., **57**.6
Miller, John C., **32**.17, **34**.19
Miller, Nathan, **41**.8
Miller, William, **8**.23, **52**.19
Mills, C. Wright, **16**.18
Mills, James Cooke, **14**.1
Mills, Robert, **19**.6
Mingay, G. E., **21**.11
Mirskey, J., **46**.21
Mitchell, Broadus, **35**.1, **78**.10, **78**.11
Mitchell, Isabel S., **22**.17
Moffatt, Walter, **68**.15
Moloney, Francis X., **22**.6
Moment, David, **66**.16
Montgomery, David, **47**.20
Moore, Charles W., **78**.12
Moore, John H., **58**.18, **62**.17, **78**.13
Moorehead, Max L., **74**.10
Morgan, Dale L., **12**.8
Morgan, Edmund S., **32**.18, **32**.19
Morgan, H. Wayne, **50**.14
Morgan, Helen, **32**.19
Morison, Samuel E., **19**.7, **36**.3, **47**.1
Morris, James A., **78**.14
Morris, Richard B., **17**.13, **28**.3, **28**.4, **53**.19, **54**.19, **54**.20, **79**.15, **81**.3
Morrison, John H., **15**.5, **70**.5
Morrison, Rodney J., **57**.7
Morriss, M. S., **26**.7
Morrow, Ralph E., **82**.6
Morse, Jarvis M., **58**.19
Morton, Richard, **19**.8
Mott, Edward H., **72**.21
Mudge, E. T., **35**.2
Mugridge, Donald H., **1**.18

Muir, Andrew F., **72**.22
Munn, Robert F., **1**.19
Munroe, John A., **36**.4
Murdoch, Angus, **66**.17
Murphy, George G. S., **6**.1
Murphy, John J., **47**.2
Musham, H. A., **70**.6
Muth, Richard F., **9**.2
Myers, Gustavus, **9**.1
Myers, Margaret G., **86**.15
Myers, Richmond E., **41**.9
Myrdal, Gunnar, **4**.14

Nadworny, Milton J., **81**.4
Nash, Gary B., **22**.7
Nash, Gerald D., **88**.14
Navin, Thomas R., **78**.15
Nelson, Daniel, **1**.20
Nerlove, Marc, **6**.2
Nettels, Curtis P., **17**.14, **26**.8, **27**.7, **29**.15, **29**.16, **29**.17, **31**.1, **31**.2, **35**.3
Neu, Irene D., **27**.8, **84**.12, **87**.11
Neufeld, Maurice, **10**.14, **36**.20
Nevins, Allan, **46**.21, **50**.15, **54**.1, **57**.8
Newcomer, Lee N., **54**.2
Niehaus, Earl F., **37**.16
Niss, James F., **65**.6
Nolen, Russell M., **81**.5
Norris, James D., **78**.16, **78**.17
Norris, Joe L., **43**.18
North, Douglass C., **3**.16, **6**.3, **6**.4, **6**.5, **7**.12, **7**.13, **7**.14, **14**.2, **43**.19, **74**.15, **86**.16
Norton, Nancy P., **77**.13
Norton, William B., **29**.18
Nussbaum, Arthur, **50**.16
Nute, Grace L., **39**.9

Oberholtzer, Ellis P., **48**.18
Ogden, Adele, **39**.10
Ohlin, Goran, **4**.15
Oliver, John W., **15**.6
Olmsted, Frederick L., **58**.2, **58**.3, **58**.4
Olsen, Bernard M., **86**.17
Olson, A. L., **21**.12
Omwake, John, **22**.18
Ostrander, Gilman M., **26**.9
Ottoson, Howard W., **39**.1
Overton, Richard C., **72**.23, **73**.1

INDEX O–R

Owen, Robert D., **67**.12

Page, Thomas W., **61**.7
Panschar, William G., **15**.7
Pares, Richard, **26**.10
Parker, P. J., **27**.9
Parker, William N., **35**.4, **62**.18, **62**.19
Parkman, Francis, **39**.11
Pate, James L., **7**.16
Patterson, Robert T., **83**.3
Paul, Rodman, W., **66**.18, **66**.19
Paxson, Frederic L., **12**.9, **73**.2
Payne, Peter L., **84**.13
Pearson, F. A., **16**.16
Pease, George B., **27**.10
Pelling, Henry, **79**.16
Pelzer, Louis, **36**.5
Perkins, Bradford, **55**.12, **55**.13
Perloff, Harvey S., **9**.2
Persons, Charles E., **81**.6
Pessen, Edward, **79**.17, **81**.7, **81**.8, **81**.9, **81**.10, **81**.11
Peterson, Arthur G., **51**.12
Peterson, Merrill, **43**.20
Phelps, Dawson A., **22**.19
Philbrick, Francis S., **12**.10
Phillips, Henry, **29**.19
Phillips, James D., **19**.9, **24**.4
Phillips, Ulrich B., **10**.15, **12**.11, **68**.16, **82**.7, **82**.8
Pierce, Bessie L., **60**.3
Pierce, Harry, H., **73**.3, **86**.18
Pinkett, Harold T., **54**.3
Pitkin, Timothy, **41**.18
Pixton, John, **73**.4
Plous, Harold J., **84**.14
Poor, Henry, **40**.7
Porter, Kenneth W., **14**.3, **35**.5
Potter, David M., **57**.4
Potter, J., **10**.16, **57**.9
Potter, Neal, **57**.2
Poulson, Barry W., **35**.6
Powell, Fred W., **71**.18
Pratt, E. J., **44**.1
Pratt, J. W., **39**.12, **55**.14
Preble, George H., **70**.7
Pred, Allan, **37**.1
Presnell, L. S., **57**.9
Preyer, Norris W., **52**.20
Price, Jacob M., **26**.11, **26**.12
Primack, M. L., **62**.20, **79**.18, **86**.19
Primm, James N., **88**.15

Puckett, Erastus P., **44**.2
Purcell, R. J., **36**.6
Purdy, T. C., **70**.8, **70**.9
Pursell, Carroll W., Jr., **15**.3
Putnam, James W., **70**.10

Ragatz, Lowell J., **44**.3
Raguet, Condy, **49**.10, **83**.13
Randall, Edwin T., **79**.19
Range, Willard, **62**.21
Ransom, James M., **22**.8
Ransom, Roger L., **70**.11, **70**.12
Rapp, Marvin A., **41**.10
Rasmussen, Wayne D., **39**.18
Ratner, Lorman, **57**.10
Ratner, Sidney, **16**.9
Rayback, Joseph G., **10**.17
Rector, William G., **66**.20
Redlich, Fritz, **3**.17, **6**.6, **6**.7, **50**.17
Reed, Merl E., **73**.5
Rees, Albert, **47**.18
Reese, Jim E., **7**.4
Reeves, Dorothea D., **2**.1
Reiser, Catherine E., **37**.2
Reiter, S., **5**.7
Remini, Robert V., **84**.15, **88**.16
Resseguie, Harry E., **87**.12
Rezneck, Samuel, **9**.3, **35**.4, **51**.13, **85**.14, **85**.15
Rhoads, Willard R., **70**.13
Rice, Otis K., **66**.21
Rich, Wesley E., **44**.4
Richter, E. E., **67**.1
Riegel, Robert E., **65**.2, **73**.6
Riemersma, Jelle C., **7**.11
Riley, Edward M., **18**.17
Ringwalt, John L., **14**.4
Ripley, William Z., **29**.20
Rippy, J. F., **44**.5
Risjord, Norman K., **55**.15
Ristow, Walter W., **40**.6
Robbins, Ray M., **39**.13, **65**.3
Robert, Joseph C., **12**.12, **39**.14, **44**.6
Roberts, Christopher, **41**.11
Roberts, William I., III, **24**.5
Robertson, Ross M., **7**.15, **7**.16
Robinson, E. A. G., **3**.4, **3**.18
Robinson, Harriet H., **78**.18
Rodrigues, J. H., **65**.4
Roeder, Robert E., **87**.13
Rogers, Tommy W., **61**.8, **61**.9
Rogin, Leo, **62**.22

INDEX
R–S

Rose, F. D., **2.2**
Rosenberg, Nathan, **76**.11, **81**.12, **85**.10
Rosenberry, Lois (Kimball) Mathews, **12**.13
Rosenblatt, Samuel M., **26**.13
Rosovsky, Henry, **4**.16, **57**.11
Ross, E. D., **12**.15
Rostow, W. W., **4**.17, **4**.18, **4**.19, **4**.20
Rothbard, Murray N., **51**.14
Rothstein, Morton, **57**.12, **63**.1, **63**.2, **63**.3, **74**.16
Rowe, Kenneth W., **35**.7
Rowe, William H., **14**.5
Rozwenc, Edwin C., **80**.1, **82**.9
Rubin, Israel I., **55**.16
Rubin, Julius, **6**.8, **37**.3, **68**.17, **69**.16
Ruffner, Ernest H., **70**.14
Russell, Robert R., **58**.20, **82**.10
Rutman, Darrett B., **19**.10
Rutter, Frank R., **44**.7
Rydell, Raymond A., **70**.15

Sachs, W. S., **17**.15, **19**.11, **21**.13, **32**.20
Sakolski, A. M., **12**.14
Sale, Randall D., **9**.4
Saloutos, Theodore, **21**.14
Salsbury, Stephen, **73**.7
Saltonstall, William G., **26**.14
Sanborn, C. H., **56**.2
Sanderlin, Walter S., **70**.16
Saraydar, Edward, **82**.11, **82**.14
Sawyer, John E., **76**.12
Scarborough, W. K., **63**.4
Schachner, Nathan, **35**.8
Schafer, Joseph, **39**.15
Schaffer, Alan, **55**.1
Scheiber, Harry N., **6**.9, **7**.17, **48**.19, **60**.4, **65**.5, **68**.13, **68**.18, **70**.17, **71**.19, **84**.16, **84**.17, **87**.14
Schleiffer, Hedwig, **2**.3
Schlesinger, Arthur M., **24**.6
Schlesinger, Arthur M., Jr., **57**.13
Schmidt, Louis B., **12**.15, **74**.17, **74**.18
Schmidt, Martin F., **47**.21
Schmookler, Jacob, **15**.8
Schneider, David M., **9**.5
Schoolcraft, Henry R., **37**.18
Schott, Joseph L., **73**.8
Schultz, Theodore, **12**.16

Schumpeter, J. A., **3**.19, **85**.16
Schur, Leon M., **84**.18
Schurr, Sam H., **76**.13
Schusler, William K., **73**.9
Schwartz, Anna J., **52**.21
Schwartz, Carol H., **85**.17
Scott, Kenneth, **29**.21
Scoville, Warren C., **21**.15
Scrivenor, Harry, **14**.13
Scroggs, William O., **84**.19
Seaman, Ezra C., **56**.11
Searight, T. B., **41**.12
Sears, Louis M., **55**.17
Sears, Marian V., **73**.10
Segal, Harvey H., **69**.12, **69**.16, **88**.6
Seligman, E. R. A., **3**.20
Sellers, Charles G., Jr., **31**.3, **84**.20
Sellers, J. B., **82**.12
Sellers, Leila, **19**.12
Setser, Vernon G., **31**.4
Severson, Robert F., Jr., **65**.6
Seybert, Adam, **33**.17
Shannon, Fred A., **65**.7
Sharp, Paul F., **65**.8
Shattuck, Lemuel, **60**.19
Shaw, Ronald E., **70**.18
Sheffield, Lord John B., **41**.19
Shepard, James, **26**.15
Sheridan, Richard B., **29**.22, **31**.5
Shipton, Clifford K., **20**.12
Shlakman, Vera, **60**.5
Shryock, Richard, **21**.16
Shultz, W. J., **16**.10
Shuman, Armin E., **70**.19
Shumway, George, **14**.6
Silberling, Norman J., **16**.11
Simon, Matthew, **71**.19
Sinclair, Harold, **60**.6
Sioussat, St. George L., **21**.17
Sirkin, Gerald, **3**.21
Sitterson, J. Carlyle, **12**.17, **63**.5
Skaggs, David C., **24**.16
Slichter, Sumner H., **9**.6
Smalley, Brian H., **74**.19
Smith, Abbot E., **20**.13, **28**.5, **28**.6
Smith, Alfred G., Jr., **58**.21
Smith, Alice E., **60**.7, **84**.21
Smith, Philip C. F., **44**.8
Smith, Thomas R., **78**.19
Smith, Walter B., **51**.15, **81**.13, **84**.22
Sobel, Robert, **51**.16
Soltow, James H., **19**.13, **24**.7
Sosin, Jack M., **31**.6, **32**.21, **32**.22
Soule, George, **7**.18

INDEX S–T

Southerland, Stella H., **17**.16, **20**.14
Sowers, Don C., **49**.1
Sparks, Earl S., **50**.18
Spaulding, E. Wilder, **37**.4
Spears, J. R., **14**.7, **28**.7
Spruill, Julia C., **28**.8
Stampp, Kenneth M., **57**.4, **82**.13
Stanchfield, Daniel, **67**.2
Standard, Diffee, **47**.3, **78**.20
Stanwood, Edward, **53**.1
Stavisky, Leonard P., **60**.8
Steinman, David B., **68**.19
Stephenson, Isaac, **67**.3
Sterns, Worthy P., **74**.20
Stettler, H. Louis, III, **77**.10
Steven, Margaret, **14**,.8
Stevens, Frank W., **73**.11
Stevens, Harry R., **37**.5, **50**.19, **65**.9
Stevens, S. K., **39**.16
Stevens, Wayne E., **22**.9
Stigler, George J., **4**.1
Still, Bayrd, **18**.17, **60**.9, **60**.10
Stilwell, Lewis D., **61**.10
Stoddard, Major Amos, **35**.14
Stoker, H. M., **16**.16
Stokes, Howard K., **16**.12
Stokes, Isaac N., **2**.4
Stover, John F., **44**.9, **73**.12
Strassmann, W. Paul, **4**.2, **47**.4, **76**.11
Stroud, Gene S., **10**.18
Studenski, Paul, **16**.13
Stuijvenberg, J. H. Van, **4**.8
Sullivan, William A., **48**.1, **80**.2, **81**.14, **81**.15
Sumner, Helen L., **79**.7
Sumner, William G., **16**.14, **49**.2
Sunder, John E., **67**.4
Supple, Barry E., **7**.19, **72**.16
Surrey, N. M. M., **26**.16
Sutch, Richard, **82**.14
Sutherland, Stella H., **20**.14
Swank, J. M., **15**.9, **15**.10
Swanson, Donald F., **49**.3
Swanson, Joseph A., **60**.17
Swartzlow, Ruby J., **39**.17
Swierenga, Robert P., **65**.10
Swisher, C. B., **84**.23
Switzler, William F., **74**.21
Sydnor, Charles S., **32**.23, **59**.1, **82**.15
Syrett, Harold C., **19**.14, **33**.18

Taber, Martha V., **47**.5
Taeuber, Conrad, **61**.11
Taeuber, Irene B., **61**.11
Taft, Philip, **48**.2
Tailby, Donald G., **55**.2
Tang, Anthony M., **9**.7
Tanner, H. S., **67**.13
Tapley, Harriet S., **24**.8
Taus, Esther R., **49**.4
Taussig, F. W., **51**.20, **53**.2
Taylor, George Rogers, 9.8, **16**.15, 30.1, 35.9, 37.15, 49.5, **51**.17, **51**.18, **55**.18, **55**.19, **57**.14, **60**.11, 65.11, 68.20, 73.16, 88.17
Taylor, Joe G., **82**.16
Taylor, Paul S., **12**.18, **20**.15, **82**.17
Taylor, Philip E., **41**.13
Taylor, Robert J., **33**.1
Taylor, Rosser H., **48**.3
Teiser, Ruth, **75**.1
Temin, Peter, **76**.14, **78**.21, **78**.22, **80**.3, **85**.18
Thayer, Theodore G., **30**.2, **33**.2
Theiss, Lewis E., **22**.10
Thernstrom, Stephan, **37**.6
Thistlewaite, Frank, **44**.10
Thomas, Brinley, **47**.16, **61**.12
Thomas, Robert P., **7**.14, **31**.7
Thompson, James H., **83**.4
Thompson, James W., **12**.19
Thompson, R. T., **36**.7, **75**.2
Thompson, Robert L., **69**.1
Thompson, Slason, **73**.13
Thompson, Warren S., **10**.19
Thompson, Wilbur R., **9**.9
Thomson, David W., **70**.20
Thomson, Robert P., **24**.9, **26**.17
Thomson, T. R., **14**.9
Thorp, Willard, **51**.19
Throckmorton, Arthur L., **87**.15
Throne, Mildred, **63**.6
Thwaites, Reuben Gold, **14**.10
Tiebout, Charles M., **4**.3
Timberlake, Richard H., Jr., **83**.5, **83**.6, **83**.7, **84**.24
Tolles, Frederick B., **24**.10
Tooker, Elva, **44**.11
Tower, Walter S., **12**.20
Towne, Marvin W., **39**.18
Tracy, George A., **48**.4
Treat, Payson J., **40**.1
Trescott, Paul B., **49**.6, **50**.20, **71**.1
Trumbull, L. R., **15**.11
Tryon, R. M., **15**.12
Tucker, George, **34**.1

INDEX

T–W

Tucker, Rufus S., **56**.12, **73**.20
Tugwell, R. G., **34**.9
Tunnell, James M., Jr., **15**.13
Tunzelmann, G. N. Von, **6**.10
Turnbull, Archibold D., **47**.6
Turner, Charles W., **73**.14
Turner, Frederick J., **65**.12
Tustin, E. B., Jr., **27**.11
Tyler, D. B., **71**.2, **79**.1
Tyler, Daniel P., **58**.10

Ubbelohde, Carl, **31**.8
Ulman, Lloyd, **81**.16
Usher, Abbott P., **15**.14

Vance, James E., Jr., **60**.12
Van Deusen, John G., **59**.2
Van Vleck, George W., **85**.19
Van Wagenen, Jared, **27**.12
Verhoeff, Mary, **22**.20
Ven Steeg, Clarence L., **17**.17, **49**.8, **54**.4
Vethake, Henry, **56**.9
Virtue, G. O., **17**.18
Von Nardroff, Ellen, **65**.13

Wade, Richard C., **37**.7, **37**.8, **82**.18
Waggoner, Madeline S., **71**.3
Wagner, Henry R., **14**.12
Wainwright, Nicholas B., **30**.3, **50**.21
Walford, Thorp L., **55**.20
Walker, Henry P., **69**.2
Walker, Joseph E., **15**.15
Wallis, George, **77**.1
Walsh, Richard, **33**.3
Walters, Raymond, Jr., **35**.10, **85**.1
Walton, Gary M., **23**.1, **23**.2, **23**.3, **26**.18
Warburton, Clark, **85**.2
Ward, David, **60**.13
Ward, G. W., **71**.4
Ware, Caroline F., **47**.7
Ware, Norman, **80**.4
Warner, Charles W., **33**.4
Warren, Charles, **53**.3
Warren, G. F., **16**.16
Warren, Winslow, **33**.5
Washburn, Wilcomb E., **33**.6
Watkins, M. H., **4**.4
Way, R. B., **40**.2, **75**.4
Weatherford, John W., **60**.14

Weaver, Glenn, **24**.11, **27**.13
Weaver, Herbert, **63**.7
Webb, Walter P., **12**.21, **65**.14
Weber, Adna F., **60**.15
Webster, Pelatiah, **49**.11
Weeden, W. B., **19**.15
Weeks, Lyman H., **15**.16
Weinberg, Albert K., **40**.3
Wells, Henry, **73**.15
Welsh, Peter C., **15**.17, **19**.16
Wender, Herbert, **75**.5
Wertenbaker, T. J., **17**.19, **19**.17, **19**.18, **21**.18, **33**.7
Wesley, Edgar B., **53**.4
Westerfield, Ray B., **44**.13
Westphall, Victor, **65**.15
Wettereau, James O., **50**.22, **50**.23
Whartenby, Franklee, **35**.4, **40**.4
Whelpton, P. K., **10**.19, **80**.5
Whitaker, Arthur P., **40**.5, **44**.14
White, Gerald T., **51**.1
White, Horace, **16**.17
White, Philip L., **23**.4, **24**.12
Whitehead, D., **76**.15
Whitehill, Walter Muir, **2**.6, **9**.12
Whitford, Noble E., **71**.5
Whitman, W. Tate, **8**.15
Whitworth, Charles, **24**.18
Whitworth, Joseph, **77**.1
Wicker, E. R., **73**.16
Wiener, Frederick B., **31**.9
Wik, Reynold M., **63**.8
Wilburn, Jean A., **85**.3
Wildes, Harry E., **44**.15
Wilkinson, Norman B., **46**.6, **47**.8
Willett, Thomas D., **85**.4
Williams, Elgin, **65**.16
Williams, John H., **73**.20
Williams, Trevor I., **14**.19
Williams, William A., **31**.10
Williamson, Harold F., **4**.5, **7**.20, **77**.9
Williamson, Jeffrey G., **43**.10, **59**.3, **60**.16, **60**.17, **75**.6, **75**.7, **75**.8
Wilson, Harold F., **37**.17, **59**.4
Wiltse, Charles M., **35**.11
Winkelman, Richard D., **65**.6
Winterbotham, William, **34**.2
Winther, Oscar O., **41**.14
Wittke, Carl F., **10**.23
Wittlinger, Carlton T., **15**.18
Wohl, R. R., **4**.6, **87**.16
Wolcott, Oliver, **49**.12
Wood, Frederic J., **41**.15

INDEX   W–Z

Wood, Frederick A., **49.**9
Wood, Gordon S, **54.**5
Wood, R. G., **67.**5
Woodbury, Levi **61.**16
Woodbury, Robert S., **47.**9, **76.**16, **76.**17
Woodfolk, George R., **44.**16
Woodman, Harold D., **10.**24, **82.**19, **87.**17
Woodward, Carl R., **12.**22
Wright, Benjamin F., Jr., **65.**17
Wright, Carroll D., **11.**1, **76.**18
Wright, Chester W., **7.**21, **53.**5
Wright, David M., **85.**5
Wright, Esmond, **17.**20
Wright, James E., **67.**6
Wright, Louis B., **17.**21, **17.**22

Wyatt-Brown, Bertram, **87.**18
Wyckoff, Vertrees J., **31.**11
Wyman, Walker D., **65.**18

Yasuba, Yasukichi, **61.**13
Yearley, Clifton K., Jr., **67.**7, **80.**6
Young, James H., **9.**13

Zahler, Helene S., **65.**19
Zartman, Lester, **86.**10
Zeis, Paul M., **44.**17
Zerchner, Oscar, **19.**19
Zevin, Robert B., **76.**19
Zilversmit, Arthur, **11.**2
Zornow, William F., **53.**6, **53.**7

Ref
Z
7165
U5T37

MAR 24 1971